2019

ANNUAL

1 3 5 7 9 10 8 6 4 2

BBC Books, an imprint of Ebury Publishing
20 Vauxhall Bridge Road,
London SW1V 2SA

BBC Books is part of the Penguin Random House group of companies whose addresses can be found at
global.penguinrandomhouse.com

Penguin
Random House
UK

Copyright © Woodland Books 2018
Text by Alison Maloney
Cover design: Two Associates
Book design: Clarkevanmeurs Design

This book is published to accompany the television series
Strictly Come Dancing first broadcast on BBC One in 2018.

Executive Producer: Louise Rainbow
Series Director: Nikki Parsons
Series Producer: Robin Lee-Perrella
Series Editor: Sarah James

With thanks to Louise Rainbow, Tessa Beckett, Selena Harvey and Jack Gledhill

First published by BBC Books in 2018

www.penguin.co.uk

A CIP catalogue record for this book is available from the British Library

ISBN 9781785942696

Printed and bound in Italy by Rotolito SpA

Penguin Random House is committed to a sustainable future for our business, our readers and our planet.
This book is made from Forest Stewardship Council® certified paper.

Picture credits: Ray Burmiston/BBC © pages 4–5, 7, 10, 13, 19, 20, 23, 26, 29, 33, 34, 37, 42, 45, 47, 52, 55, 59, 60,
63, 64, 66, 69, 71, 72, 75, 82, 85, 87, 88, 91, 96, 99, 104, 107,110, 113, 116, 119, 123, 125, 127, 128;
Sarah James © page 48; Patrick Doherty design © pages 108–9. Guy Levy/BBC © page 9, 24, 30–1, 50–1,
56, 76–8, 80–1, 92–3, 100–3, 120–1; Shutterstock © page 94; Getty © page 95; All images on pages 14–17 and 39–41
provided by the respective dancer or singer. All other images © BBC.

2019

ANNUAL

BBC
BOOKS

CONTENTS

Over the next few weeks, Claudia Winkleman will watch wide-eyed as the competing couples pull dance after dance out of the bag. But she says there is one dance that never fails to give her goosebumps – the opening number of the series.

'I love it when the *Strictly* pros take to the floor for the first time,' she says. 'You see the audience's faces light up. They are the best at what they do and when all their feet hit the dance floor, I get the shivers and get a bit goosebumpy.'

The presenter always has a ball on camera, but she reveals that the Friday rehearsal has thrown up some truly memorable moments.

'My favourite moments are always when a member of the crew gets on the radio and says, "Come and see this." We're all quite busy but often on a Friday we get a call "to the floor" and that means someone is doing a brilliant or hilarious routine. It happened a lot with Ed Balls, when he did "Gangnam Style" and when Oti did her African Samba with Danny Mac. Those moments are littered throughout the series.'

Although it's early days for the class of 2018, Claudia says her first impressions are promising.

'The celebrities are a joy,' she says. 'They feel happy, bouncy, excitable. I think we're going to have a good time with them. The first time I saw them together they already felt confident to me. Sometimes at that stage there are a few who are nervous, but they threw themselves into the moves with gusto.

'I'm slightly obsessed by the girls this year. They all look like they are just here to have a good time, which is all you want.

'I love Kate Silverton. She told me, "I am SO out of my comfort zone," but I told her she would be fine, and she will be. I have watched her read the news for years and I've always respected her. She's a smart cookie and she can't wait to be *Strictlified*.

'There were so many wonderful moments last year,' she says. 'But I loved the Revd. Richard Coles. He was really funny and the sight of him descending from the heavens on a cloud was brilliant.

'Debbie McGee surprised me. In the first shows she was so nervous that her whole body was trembling, and she went on to make the Final. I loved last year's Final – when Joe won, I was happy for Katya because she looked over the moon and she'd put together such an amazing routine.'

Claudia is as excited as ever for a new series, 'I love being behind the scenes and I love all our producers. We have been together now for six years and have the most brilliant time. When we have a script meeting we have to add extra time so we can all chat, hug and share photos of dogs, babies or whatever. I love Tess, and we always have a great time. For me, it's the people who make the show.

'The reunion for the first week is lovely because it is like a family and we're all so happy to see each other and catch up. We're like that for a couple of weeks, then, as people start to learn how to dance and accomplish something that they're really proud of, that they couldn't have done in week one, you start to feel like you are going along on their journey with them.'

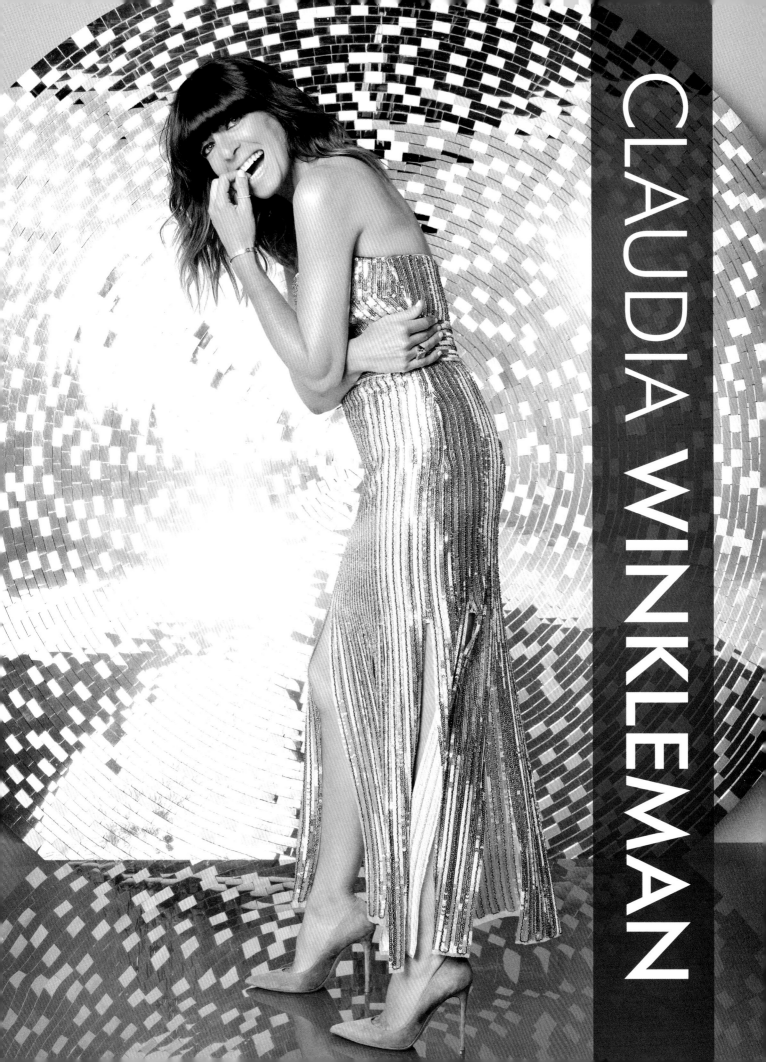

CLAUDIA WINKLEMAN

DOCTOR OF DANCE

When *Holby City* star Joe McFadden swapped his scrubs for sequins, he had little previous dance experience and, he says, 'Winning was the furthest thing from my mind.' So being crowned the *Strictly* champ in the 2017 Grand Final was a very special moment.

'It was the most amazing and surprising thing that could have happened,' says Joe. 'Looking back at that moment will always be a source of joy to me.'

Joe, who danced to victory with Katya Jones, admits his lack of prowess on the dance floor made him reluctant to sign up.

'When I first met up with Louise Rainbow, the Executive Producer, I said I loved the show, but the dancing in previous series was of such a high standard, I just couldn't imagine getting to that point. She said, "Don't worry. You just have to show up and show willing and the professional will get you there." That's what Katya did, somehow.

'It's a difficult mission for the professionals. They have to be amazing dancers and brilliant choreographers, as well as teaching complete beginners. They bring out the best in us and they are the real stars of the show.

'Katya's work ethic is astounding and her dedication rubbed off on me. I looked round at the beginning and said, "I'm not as good as so many people here." She said, "Don't look at other people, look at yourself. It doesn't matter where you are at this point, just that you get better every week."'

The Scottish actor admits that nerves got the better of him in the early weeks.

'The first dance, a Jive, was the purest form of fear that I've ever felt,' he said. 'When my name was announced I thought, "I can't do this! There's been a terrible mistake." But it went so well, I thought I had it nailed. Then the second week was just as terrifying and our Tango was terrible. I realised it wasn't going to get any less nerve-wracking. But the show taught me that you can feel that fear and still go on and do it.'

After scoring 22 for the Tango, Joe's marks improved week after week, but it was week eight, he believes, before he truly hit his stride.

'It all started to come together after the Rumba,' he says. 'It is a notoriously difficult dance and we got a couple of nines. Because it had been so challenging and gone so well, I felt like it was all finally clicking into place. The next week I got to do my Salsa at Blackpool, which was phenomenal. From that point I understood why people enjoy dancing so much.'

Another highlight was Joe's Musicals-Week Samba to 'Money, Money' from *Cabaret*.

'Katya's choreography was amazing. I was playing the MC in *Cabaret*, which is a brilliant character, and I thought, "This is why I wanted to do this show."'

Joe was buoyed by the huge public support,

especially in his hometown of Glasgow, where he met fans towards the end of the series.

'You're practising in a rehearsal room for 15 weeks, so meeting the people who watch the show was brilliant. The public support helped us perform that bit better. On the Live Tour we went back to Glasgow and played the SSE Hydro and people were cheering me and fellow Glaswegian Susan Calman on. There was so much noise, we felt like rock stars!'

Going from non-dancer to *Strictly* champ requires dedication, and Joe says anyone coming into the show needs to 'be prepared to work the hardest you ever have'.

'It's the most demanding thing I've ever done and will ever do, both physically and emotionally, but it's also the most rewarding. I envy anyone going into the next series because they are going to have the most amazing time.'

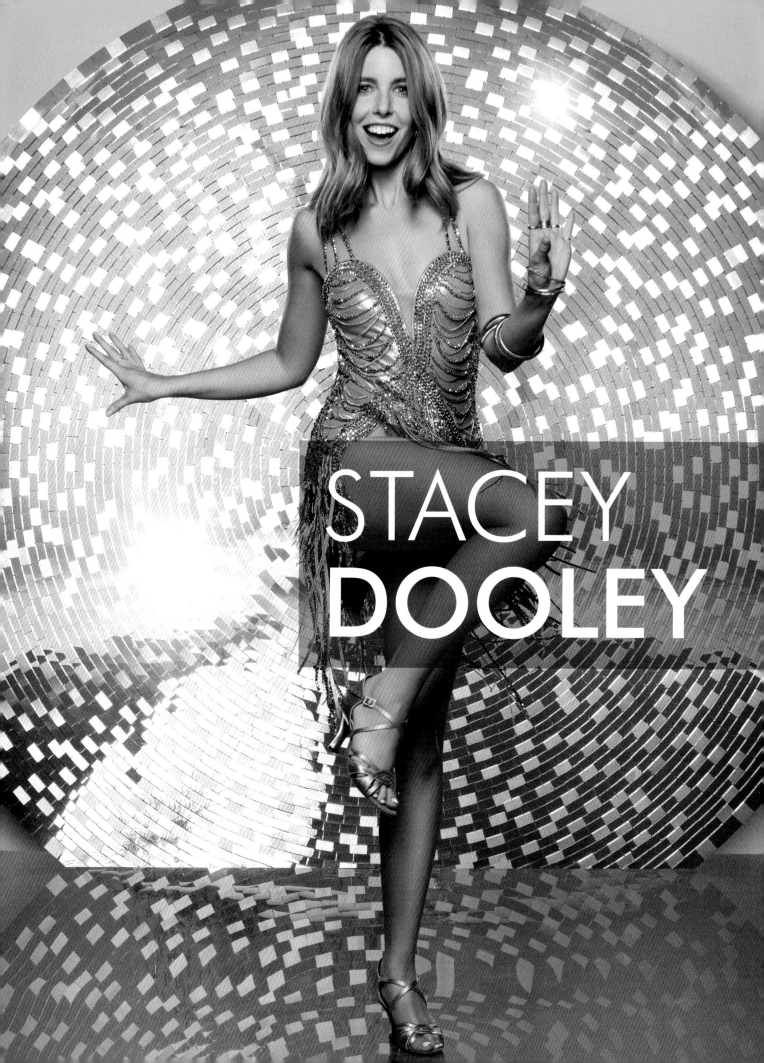

STACEY
DOOLEY

Fans of Stacey Dooley's award-winning documentaries are used to seeing her grappling with gritty subjects, from sweatshops to extremism. But she is looking forward to letting her hair down and showing her fun side on the dance floor.

'I have always loved the show,' says Stacey. 'I think it's brilliant that it's something the whole family can be involved with and also you're learning a genuine skill.

'My work is so heavy and it's quite hardcore, and it can be quite harrowing at times, so Strictly is total escapism. It's a real treat in that sense, dancing and enjoying myself and just celebrating that side of me. My day-to-day work is serious, so you don't necessarily associate me with jumping around, dancing.'

Stacey's TV career began at the age of 21, when she appeared in the documentary Blood, Sweat and T-shirts, exposing the use of child labour in the fashion industry. That led to her own series, Stacey Dooley Investigates, which saw her tackling social issues all over the world, from her hometown of Luton to Japan, the Congo, Thailand, Kenya and Cambodia.

'I've travelled extensively for 10 years and been so privileged in so many ways,' she says. 'But Strictly is one of the most amazing things I've ever done. It is so crazy and fun. The clothes are amazing, it's a lovely crowd, you're dancing, you're learning a skill and you're on a high.

'It's all mad! For the red-carpet event I was in a gold leotard. I would never dress in a gold leotard! I used to work at Luton Airport selling perfume and there was one which had a curvy gold bottle. My friend texted me and said, "You look like that perfume." But it's great fun.'

Out of all the dances, Stacey – who is partnered by Kevin Clifton – is especially keen to try the Tango.

'I'm quite clumsy and a bit all over the shop, so it will be quite nice to see if I can do a considered, definite routine. I also quite fancy the Charleston as well, because it's fast and furious.'

Four-time finalist Kevin Clifton is thrilled to partner investigative journalist Stacey Dooley in this series.

'I've been watching her documentaries for years and I'm a big fan, which is why I was so excited when we got partnered up,' he says. 'As a person, Stacey's not what I expected at all. She's like a kid with loads of energy. I think she's got more energy than me, which is saying something. She's really happy and jokey, so she definitely has a massive fun side to her. I want everybody to see the fun Stacey.'

In the first few weeks of training Stacey was working on another TV show, so the couple had to snatch a few hours here and there to train but he's happy with her progress.

'She's doing great,' he says. 'A lot of the moves are completely alien to her, so I am having to explain in detail what everything is and what I want her to do, but she's throwing herself in and she's really enthusiastic, so that makes my job easier. She wants to learn and she's a really positive person.'

Stacey has already unveiled her signature move.

'On the red carpet someone asked her if she had any moves she would do in a club and she did what has now been christened a "Dooley Drop", when she drops down to the floor and up again. I don't think there will be any of that in our routines, but we'll see!'

'Kevin from Grimsby', as he was affectionately dubbed by Sir Bruce Forsyth, was taught by his parents, former World Champions Keith and Judy Clifton, from an early age. He was a Youth World Number One and four-time British Latin Champion, as well as winning International Open titles in 14 countries.

Kevin joined *Strictly* in 2013 and is the only professional dancer to reach four consecutive Grand Finals, with Susanna Reid, Frankie Bridge, Kellie Bright and Louise Redknapp. Last year he had an impressive run with Susan Calman.

'Susan said, "I just don't want to be the first one to go. If I can make it past the first elimination, I'll be really happy." Once we got past that, we decided to treat every week like our last and have a great time. But every week we kept getting through.'

While they left in week 10, the couple took part in the *Strictly Come Dancing Live* tour and won – beating all four finalists, including champ Joe McFadden.

'We danced the Wonder Woman Samba and the Morecambe and Wise Quickstep and she got a massive reception every night. She was enjoying it so much and then she began to improve and we just started winning. At the end it was between us and Debbie McGee and it came down to the last show – and we won. We couldn't believe it.

'So finally I have a glitterball. After Susanna, Frankie, Kellie and Louise, it was Susan Calman that won me the glitterball!'

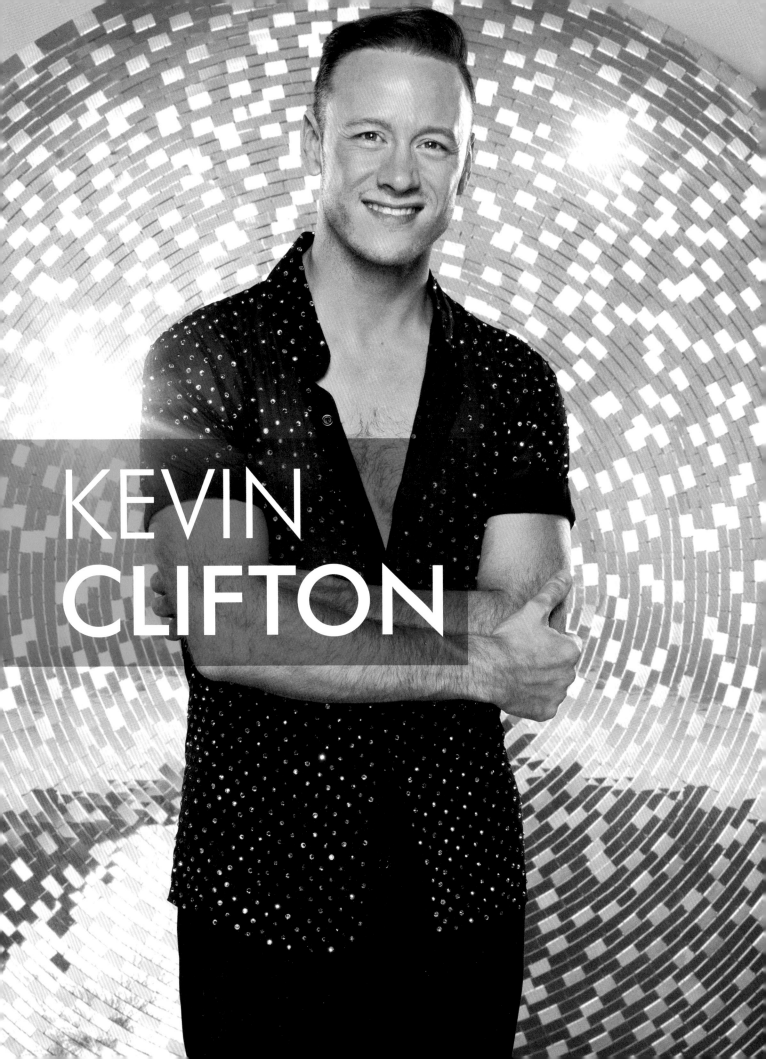

KEVIN
CLIFTON

WHO'S THE CUTIE?

Strictly's brilliant professional dancers have been honing their skills since they were knee-high to a Lindy Hopper. They're all grown-up now, but they have shared their throwback pictures so you can see just how cute they were when they started out, and the advice they would like to give their younger selves. Can you guess which pro is which?

1

'The joy you feel when you dance will last you a lifetime. The pain of stretching will be worth it, the late rehearsals will pay off and the tears you shed for the parts you didn't get will dry. You have such a wonderful career ahead of you and the places that you see and the people you meet along the way will make all of the bad moments so much better. So dance for the fun of it and don't forget to remember the feeling of expressing what you love.'

'Enjoy every second of the good, the bad and the ugly. This will make you a success, but you always have to remember to give back.'

'Always trust and listen to your inner self.'

'Don't be afraid to dream and dream big! The road to achieving your dreams is going to have many ups and downs, but never lose sight of the end goal. The blood, sweat and tears are all worth it, because when those dreams become a reality, there really is no greater feeling. Don't give up. Keep pushing, keep fighting, because I promise you it's worth it.'

'Listen up, *bambino*. You were born to win, baby. Be strong, stay focused and remember that dance is life.'

'The advice I would give to myself is to do it the same way all over again. Everything in my life has happened for a reason and has led me into all these amazing paths and experiences that have shaped me into the person I am today.'

'Work hard, don't take shortcuts and KEEEEEP DANCING!'

8

'Not everything will go as you've always planned, but always trust and believe in yourself and your gut. It will be your navigator in life.'

9

'Don't be afraid to dream and be unique, because that's what makes me and everyone else special.'

10

'Always keep learning, as you never know where life will take you. Always work hard, as it will always be worth it. Do what you love and keep smiling, even if you're missing teeth!'

12

'Don't let anyone change your choices because they don't think you're right. There will be very hard times, a lot of sacrifices and unavoidable mistakes, which are there to make you stronger. Keep being you and keep working hard no matter how tough things may get. Trust me, one day it will all be worth it! So, so worth it!'

11

'Cherish every moment and trust that in the end your dreams will come true.'

13

'It's OK to be yourself, the world will adjust. Despite where you come from, your dreams are valid. Know that you're worthy of greatness and always have courage to tell your truth. Honour your feelings and continue to value relationships over things. Give back and be grateful. Believe in yourself and trust your light. The tide will turn and life will be more amazing than you ever thought possible.'

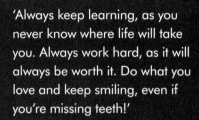

'Never stop following your dream. If the goal is clear in your mind, nobody can stop you. Everything is possible, and now I really can say that I am a pro dancer in one of the best TV shows I know. I'm so proud of my younger self!'

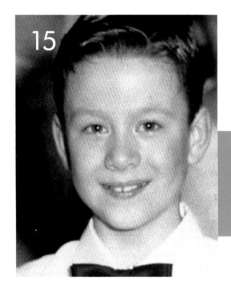

'Don't worry too much about everyone else's opinion of you. Work hard, know your own worth and make happiness your goal. Remember, the key to any art is not about doing nothing wrong, it's about doing something magical.'

'Always follow your dreams, and fight for them. Don't let anyone or anything stop you from what you want to do in life. If you really want something, just believe in yourself and work hard and with passion, and you'll get it. There's nothing worse than regretting something and knowing that you didn't do everything that you could. So always give your best to fight for your dreams.'

'Once upon a time I was a little girl with big dreams who promised to herself she would make them real one day, and so I did. I'm sure you can do it too, so follow your dreams, believe in yourself and never, ever give up.'

If the latest batch of *Strictly* contestants want to impress Bruno Tonioli, they will have to do two things.

'I want to be surprised and excited, and it's up to them to do it,' he explains. 'That's really the key to *Strictly*. Show me something that reinvents the dance every time, that keeps it fresh and relevant. Show me an angle I haven't seen before. I want to continue to be surprised and awestruck by what they come up with and, to be fair, they always do that.'

The Italian judge has already warmed to the new recruits and says there was more enthusiasm than nerves at the launch show.

'Obviously, until they do the first live show they will be nervous, because it's a big thing to take on, but I felt they were willing to go for it and enjoy the experience, which I liked.'

What do you make of the line-up?

They are a very good, fresh, keen cast. They have a great energy. They are very enthusiastic, all out there, going for it. There is scope for a lot of interesting things to happen.

How did they do in their first group dance?

It's difficult to assess them on the first dance. Quite a few seemed to have a natural aptitude and there were a few faux pas, but I'm not going to name names! Some seemed to take to it like ducks to water and a few looked like rhinoceroses charging, but give them a chance and they will get better.

Do you have your eye on anyone?

Charles has got something. He's very charismatic and has a strong presence. Vick and Graziano make a great couple, so I'm expecting a lot. I'm excited about all the new pros. They are really good, really keen and energetic.

Anyone else you are looking forward to watching?

Lauren will really go for it, I think. Dancing is a very different challenge, but I'm sure Lauren is going to give it all she's got.

What was your favourite moment of last year?

Debbie McGee's Argentine Tango was absolutely sublime. That was one of the best Argentine Tangos we've seen. It was absolutely stunning.

What did you make of the Final?

It was very close last year. All of them were great and the margin was so small – at least between the final four. I could not have called it.

What did you make of Shirley's debut?

She was very, very good. She knows what she's talking about, she's honest in her opinion and it's based on her experience, which is considerable. More of the same, please.

What is your favourite week?

The Final is always exciting, people have worked so hard to get there and usually they come up with the best dances. I like the themed weeks, like Movie Week, Musicals and Halloween, when there is a bit more range in creativity. But surprises happen every week. With *Strictly*, you never know what you are going to get!

BRUNO TONIOLI

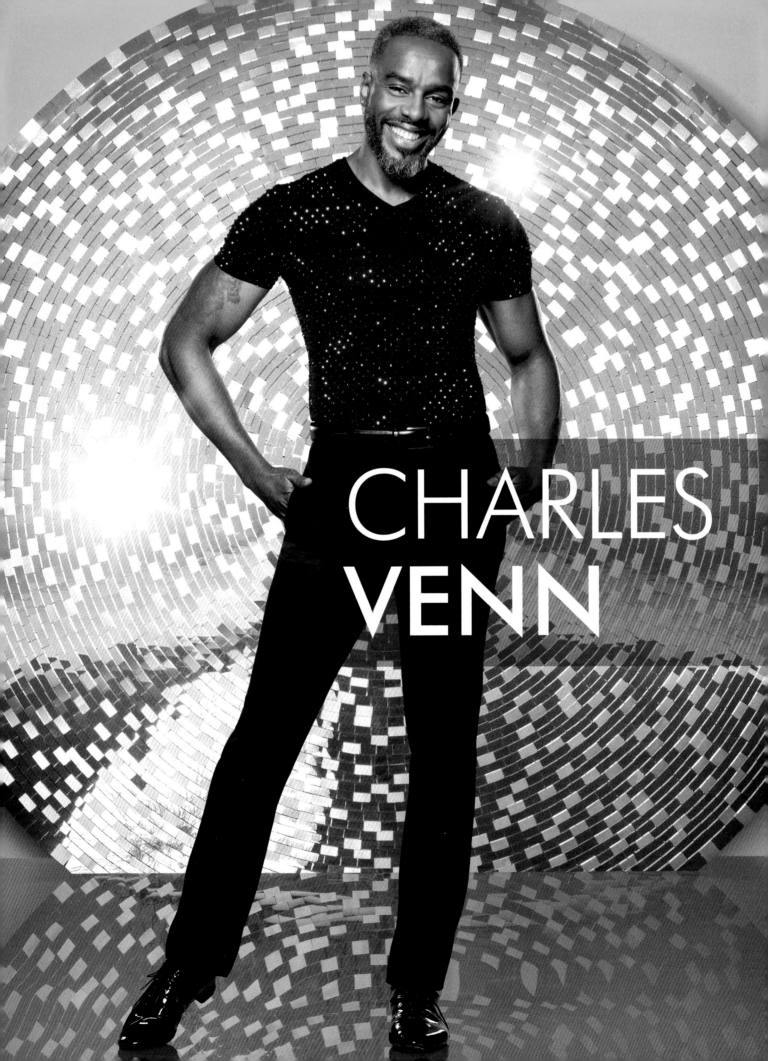

CHARLES
VENN

Casualty and *Holby City* have produced *Strictly* winners in the past, including champions Joe McFadden and Tom Chambers. But how does *Casualty* star Charles Venn rate his chances?

'I'd like to think I've got rhythm,' he says. 'In terms of rating my dancing, I would say I'm probably a six. Still four more to go.'

Charles grew up in London and went to a performing arts college as a teenager. After starring in the football dramas *Dream Team* and *Footballers' Wives*, he played the role of Ray Dixon in *EastEnders* between 2011 and 2013. Two years later he joined the cast of *Casualty* as nurse Jacob Masters.

After signing up for *Strictly*, Charles was given plenty of advice from former co-stars who had appeared on the show.

'I spoke to Chizzy Akudolu and my *EastEnders* co-star Tameka Empson,' he said. 'They told me, "This is huge, this is an amazing gig. You're going to have so much fun." They said, "Try not to take yourself too seriously and enjoy the moment." That was the best advice they gave me and I'm trying to do that.

'The *Casualty* cast were so excited when I finally revealed the news to them. I had to keep the secret for a month and a half and when it came out they were all, "Oh my God, you're doing *Strictly!* That's fantastic."'

As he is still filming the show, Charles and pro partner Karen Clifton will have a packed schedule, splitting their time between London and Cardiff, but he takes it all in his stride.

'Life is all about challenges,' he says. 'Many people would dream of doing such a gig, so I'm living in the moment and enjoying it. But I'm testing myself in a way I've never done before, so ask me how I feel in a couple of months' time!'

The actor, who has Nigerian heritage, thinks he will be more suited to the Latin party dances than the ballroom but is excited about trying both.

'I'm an African man,' he says. 'We use our hips because that's just what we do. So for me, Salsa, snake hips, all day, that's fine. That's fun. But this Foxtrot stuff and the Jive – that feels like learning how to walk again and it's pretty daunting.

'But I'm excited, nervous, experiencing butterflies, all in equal measure. I can't wait to get my first dance out there.'

And he's looking forward to getting into the *Strictly* vibe, with sparkles and sequins galore.

'Let's go!' he laughs. 'You've got to embrace it. If you're self-conscious, you are in the wrong business!'

For this series of *Strictly*, Karen Clifton will be spending a lot of time in A&E – but only because she has been paired with *Casualty* star Charles Venn. The actor is fitting his rehearsals around filming, and that means spending most of the week in Cardiff.

'We will be travelling back and forth to Cardiff a lot,' says Karen. 'But that's fine, because I'm used to travelling for the rehearsals. His schedule is going to be pretty tough, so we'll try to make the most out of it. Anywhere that I can get him training, I will. I won't waste any time. Even if he's on set, we'll be rehearsing between scenes.

'When I'm not there he is sending me videos of him practising, which is a good thing. I really love when somebody is as committed as that, and he is enjoying it as well, so that's an added bonus. He's a lovely guy and he's got a great energy about him.'

Karen was born in Venezuela and moved to New York when she was eight years old. She is Professional World Mambo Champion. She joined *Strictly* in 2012, and partners have included Mark Wright, whom she took to the Grand Final, and Jeremy Vine.

This year she is hoping to get to the Final for a second time and she says her pupil shows promise.

'Charles is extremely enthusiastic and very focused,' she says. 'I've been lucky that I've had some amazing partners in the past that have always wanted to work hard, and Charles is fantastic already. We get along really well. Plus, he's an actor and I guess being in the performance world he gets into it straight away.

'I'm not taking it easy with him. The great thing is, he is very fit and he can connect his mind to his body. Dance is something that is foreign to him, but he is definitely up for the challenge.'

Karen thinks Charles will gravitate towards the Latin dances, but she is optimistic for the ballroom, too.

'Charles has natural rhythm, which is great and always comes in handy when doing the Latin dances. But when we come to the ballroom dances he might surprise me and he might surprise himself – ballroom may turn out to be his forte. Watch this space.'

Last year Karen danced with *Sunday Brunch* star Simon Rimmer – who found that the way to this girl's heart was through her stomach.

'I loved Simon,' she laughs. 'He is a gentle soul and brought me food all the time, which is a good way to be the teacher's pet!

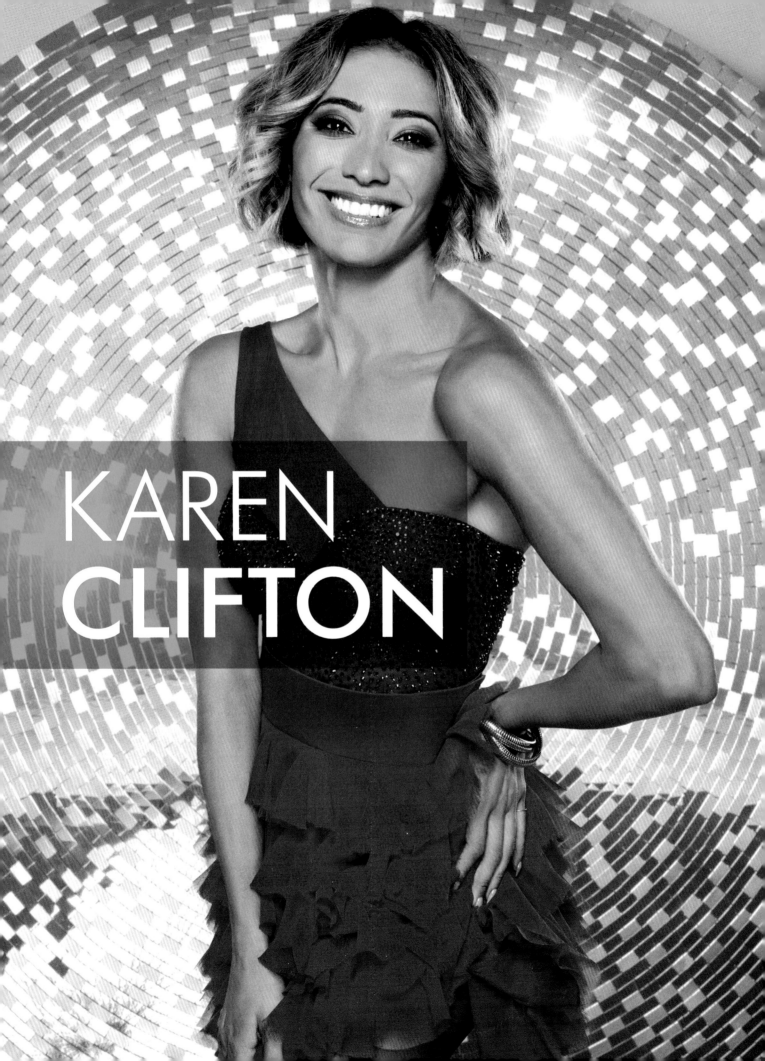

KAREN
CLIFTON

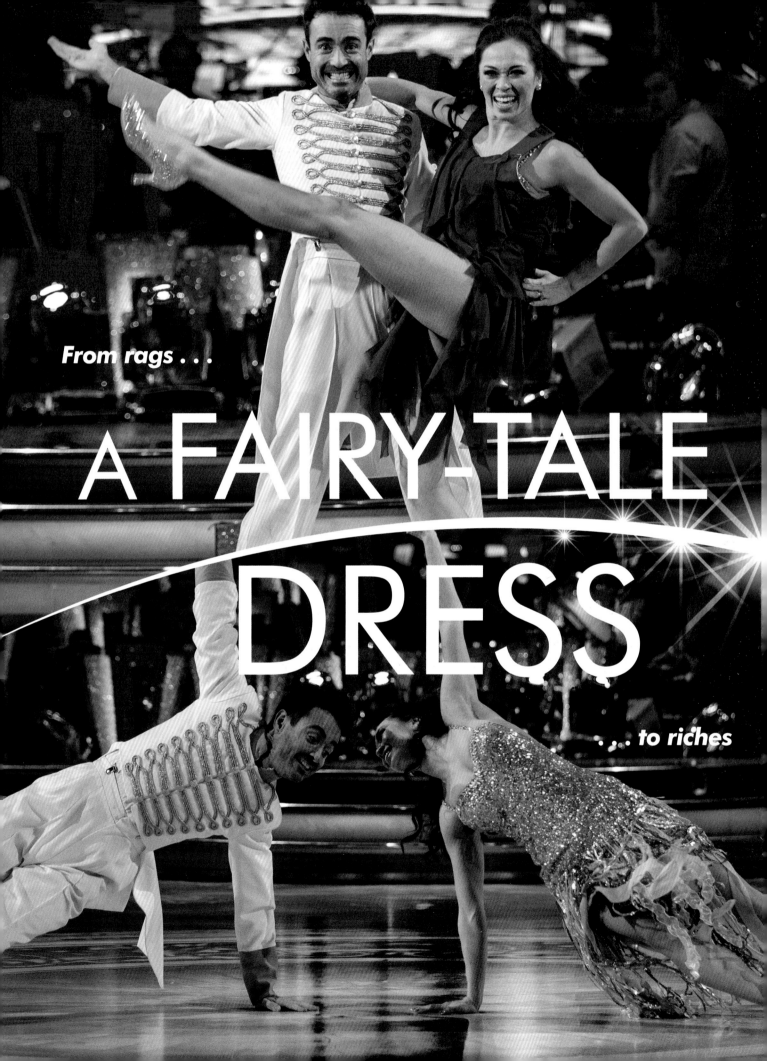

From rags . . .

A FAIRY-TALE DRESS

. . . to riches

Joe McFadden's *Cinderella*-themed showdance, with Katya Jones, cast a spell on the audience and played a part in him winning the title of 2017 *Strictly* champ.

But it wasn't just Prince Charming's dashing dancing that enchanted viewers. Katya's magical transformation from ballroom queen to kitchen maid and back to sparkly princess left everyone spellbound.

Katya began the dance, to Hall & Oates's 'You Make My Dreams', wearing a blue dress, but, as the clock struck midnight, she ran from her prince's arms and reappeared in grey rags. Then, mid-twirl, with a twinkle of the fairy's wand, Katya's rags morphed into a silver, sequinned gown fit for a princess.

The unforgettable costume was created by *Strictly*'s costume designer Vicky Gill, after Katya came to her with the idea.

'Katya had done something similar in her own dance show,' reveals Vicky. 'But on stage they have two-and-a-half-minute routines and we had 90 seconds for three changes, so it was a big ask. From the blue rip-off to the change of sparkly shoes, and the final drop-down, there was a lot that could go wrong. But I was confident that together we'd find a way.'

Vicky can now reveal the secret behind the fairy-tale dress. 'Katya started with a blue overdress, which was concealing everything else,' she says. 'It was bulky – but for that fleeting moment the silhouette was right.

'The back of the dress had a section of Velcro down the centre. When Katya ran up the stairs, a wardrobe assistant, Megan, was at the top to rip it off. That revealed the charcoal grey rag inspired dress.'

Then came the tricky part – the transformation from rags to riches before the audience's very eyes.

'The rag dress had a section of sequins rolled up on the hip,' explains Vicky. 'The upper section housed all of the sequinned top and fringed skirt for the final dress, which rolled up, and the whole thing was disguised by the rags dress. It was still quite voluminous, but the movement of the dress as she twirled concealed it.

'It was secured at the shoulder with elastic and Velcro, but not too much because if it sticks you lose that quick release.

'At the crucial moment, Katya had to release it from the shoulders and then push the material down. Everything from her bustline to her hips tumbled down to become the skirt and the fringing and the sequins on the top half were revealed. Katya had to use some force to push it down while she spun, to make sure it was fluid and didn't get stuck, which would spoil the moment.'

Although the design was tried and tested, Vicky admits to a few nerves on the night.

'We were confident it was going to work,' she says. 'But we were watching on the monitor backstage and I couldn't even look at the screen. I asked the floor manager to let me know when the dress was rolled down, and the feeling of relief when he said, "It's down," was amazing. Everyone in the room was over the moon. We had pulled it off!

'It was a fairy-tale ending to a brilliant series.'

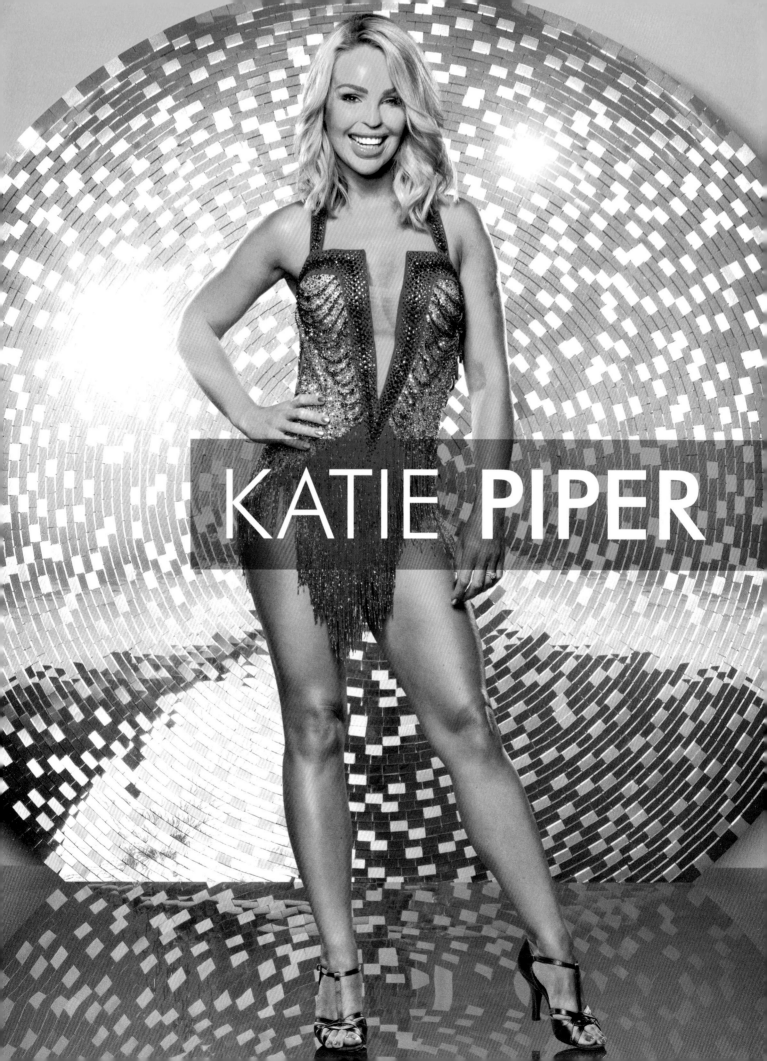

KATIE PIPER

TV presenter Katie Piper is eager to learn to dance and claims she is slightly challenged in the dance department.

'I'm not even on the scale, seriously, I'm not,' she says. 'I'm so bad that I can't even clap to the beat when I'm watching a musical.'

Katie, from Andover, Hampshire, was an aspiring model when she became the victim of an acid attack in 2008 that caused severe burns to her face and body and left her blind in one eye. Following the attack, Katie underwent over 60 operations, including pioneering reconstruction surgery, and regained her sight. As a result, she set up the Katie Piper Foundation to help burns victims and appeared in a documentary, *Katie: My Beautiful Face*, which led to more TV work, including *Bodyshockers*. She has also written several books including her two autobiographies *Beautiful* and *Beautiful Ever After*.

Now a happy mum and busy TV star, Katie is looking forward to learning a new skill.

'*Strictly* is a totally new challenge,' she says. 'It's something I've never done before and it's totally new territory, and I really believe in pushing yourself and taking on new challenges. But my main reason for taking part is that it's actually fun and something that I'm excited about, excited to talk about and I'm going to learn something new. No matter how far I get, I'll notice a big change in myself that will continue after the show.'

The TV star will dance with Gorka Márquez and says she hopes learning to dance will boost her confidence.

'I hope Gorka will teach me how to be confident when moving and dancing on the floor, but I'm sure he can help me have fun with it, too.'

As mum to a four-year-old and a baby, Katie says her biggest challenge will be finding time to practise.

'I'm going to try to commit as much time as possible,' she says. 'The struggle won't be other work but more my role as a mum, because I have two girls. One was only born in December 2017, but my oldest girl loves dancing, so I'll try to involve her and get her excited about it.'

In the meantime, Katie is getting excited about her *Strictly* makeover.

'That's one part that I'm going to revel in,' she says. 'I'm quite a glamorous person and I love tanning and make-up, so I'm going to be so excited by that. I've had a costume fitting and that was so cool, because you think, "Where else would I ever get to wear this?!"'

Last year, Gorka Márquez came within inches of lifting the trophy after dancing his way to the Final with Alexandra Burke. This year, he is partnered with presenter and author Katie Piper.

'I was super-excited to be paired with Katie,' he says. 'She is such an inspirational woman and to be able to work with her and get to know her better is really inspiring for me. She has such a strong personality and I think she is incredible. It gives me more motivation and I really want to do well for her.'

Gorka believes she has got what it takes to make it on the show.

'She is very excited and a little bit nervous, because it is out of her comfort zone, but she's doing well,' he says. 'She is very enthusiastic and throwing herself into the routines. She's very positive, very happy and, for someone who has never danced before, she has made a great start.'

Because of initial nerves, the Spanish pro believes ballroom might be Katie's forte, at least until her confidence grows.

'From what she has told me I think she will enjoy the ballroom and I think she might feel safer when she is in hold.

'I will try to make her feel comfortable and the best thing to do is to give her moves she feels happy with and see what works well. Hopefully she will soon feel more confident and will enjoy the dance.'

As the new series begins, Gorka is hoping it's third time lucky, but he reckons he has some stiff competition.

'It's early days, but there are so many people who could do very well,' he says. 'It's going to be a great season. I can't wait.'

'Everyone wants to get into the Final, and in my second series, to get to the Final and get almost all 10s, was incredible,' says Gorka. 'Dancing with Alexandra was amazing. She is such a talented person.'

Gorka began dancing at the age of 12 and represented his native Spain in the World Latin Championships in 2010, as well as reaching the Semi-finals of the 2012 WDSF World Cup. He joined *Strictly* in 2016, dancing with Tameka Empson in his first season.

GORKA MÁRQUEZ

SPOT THE
DIFFERENCE

You've got an eye for a great dance, but how is your attention to detail? Do you have the eagle eyes of Shirley, Craig, Bruno and Darcey when it comes to spotting the little things that make a big difference? This image of Aston Merrygold's Salsa has been duplicated with 10 tiny changes. How many can you spot? Turn to page 128 to find the answers . . .

Since she last graced the *Strictly* judging panel, Darcey Bussell has become a dame The former prima ballerina, who picked up her gong in May 2018, said she was 'shocked' to be awarded the well-deserved honour. But now it's back to the day job and Dame Darcey couldn't be more excited.

'At the launch show we all looked at each other and said, "It can't possibly have been eight months." But as always, I get a little buzz in my tummy, a ball of excitement. I think it's going to be a great series. The best yet.'

What do you think of the line-up?

It is incredibly exciting. They seem like a bunch who are raring to go and already really fit. We've got a really entertaining group that are very conscious of the world of *Strictly*, they are ready and willing and have that buzz where they all want to be winners. There will be the natural nerves, but, as a group, it looks like we are going to have a great first couple of shows.

Have you got your eye on anyone in particular?

There are lots of celebrities this year who I believe could do incredibly well. Ashley Roberts and Lee Ryan spring to mind, and Danny John-Jules could be exceptional. He's a character and he's a fit gentleman. Vick Hope could be great. Lauren Steadman is an incredibly fit, beautiful girl, and nothing will get in her way. She's fearless, so AJ will be able to throw her around.

Who might surprise you?

Possibly Stacey Dooley. Stacey and Kevin will be fun together. Joe Sugg could be surprising, he has eight million followers on YouTube, but it's very different being on the dance floor with the audience right in there front of you.

Who might provide the laughs?

Seann Walsh is hysterical. He's so excited. He's going to be great and Katya will be able to get the best out of him and work with his strengths, just as she did with Ed Balls.

What was your favourite moment of last year?

There were many, but I love that Debbie McGee did really well. It was something that was incredibly special to her and you really sensed that. She and Giovanni did some fantastic things, and the Viennese Waltz was beautiful. Joe and Katya's Argentine Tango was daring and unusual and we had Susan Calman. I couldn't get enough of watching her. It shows how rounded the show is.

DARCEY BUSSELL

VICK HOPE

As a DJ, Vick Hope loves music, but she insists that doesn't make her a natural dancer.

'I love dancing, although it doesn't mean that I'm particularly good at it,' she says. 'At Capital radio, whenever we're playing songs I literally throw myself around the studio. I like to move to music and I've broken chairs, a bit of the wall, spilt coffee everywhere!'

Vick grew up in Newcastle upon Tyne and went to Cambridge University, where she earned a degree in modern languages. She worked for music channels such as MTV and 4Music, and in May 2017 she took over Capital's breakfast show with co-presenter Roman Kemp.

Strictly, she says, is a chance to start learning something new again.

'During your younger years, you're learning all the time,' she explains. 'You go to school, maybe go to university or some kind of higher education or training, and then it all stops because you get a job and you have to support yourself and pay your rent. So you forget that learning is such a stimulating experience.

'It's so rare that you get an opportunity like this and I'm really grateful that it's dance, because it's my favourite thing in the world. It just makes me happy. As soon as you hit the dance floor, I feel like you don't think about anything else, so I'm having the most fun.'

Although she's in a happy place, Vick – who is paired with new dancer Graziano Di Prima – admits she is nervous of the judges.

'We're doing this thing that we've never done before and being judged on it by the best in the world,' she says. 'It's a mad situation and I am scared, but I want them to to give us pointers that we can take forward to get better.'

One thing the judges might want to look out for is Vick's facial expressions.

'I have an over-expressive face,' she says. 'I move my eyebrows too much, especially when the cameras are rolling. It's really malleable and looks a bit like plasticine. At the red-carpet launch I look overanimated in every picture. I was so happy, I couldn't stop smiling, but I realise that it was just a little bit too much. I'm going to practise a smile that's not so intense.'

New recruit Graziano Di Prima is over the moon to be joining *Strictly* and says it is a 'dream come true'. 'I'm very excited,' he says. 'I always watched Strictly and I used to dream of being there with all the dancers, and now I am here, and it's unbelievable. The first time I danced with the group was amazing. To be on the stage with the guys, the audience, the camera. The feeling was "wow".'

The Italian dancer knew fellow Sicilian Giovanni Pernice from the dance school in Bologna where they both trained as teenagers, but he says all the professionals have welcomed him with open arms.

'They are amazing,' he says. 'Already they are more than family for me. During group rehearsals we spend so many hours together and it's always fun.'

Graziano grew up in a small town in Sicily and started competing at six. 'I'm from a supportive family,' he says. 'My dad ran a vineyard and I am the only one who dances, so they did everything for me to help me grow and follow my dream.'

At 17, he moved to Bologna to study dance. He made the top 24 at the under-21 Latin World Championships. He found fame on the Italian talent show *Amici di Maria de Filippi* before turning professional and joining the cast of *Burn the Floor*, which he says 'changed my life because I got to go around the world and dance'.

For his *Strictly* debut, Graziano has been partnered with DJ Vick Hope, and he's delighted.

'Vick is the best partner I could have. I think Vick will be better at the Latin. The Samba, Jive, Salsa – all the fast dances – will be good for her, but she will have to get used to doing everything and I think she will be good at the ballroom too. If she can keep the frame, she will do well. She will be on top of her game.'

But she'd better be prepared to knuckle down. Graziano has already warned her that he takes his tutoring very seriously.

'As a person I am funny, but when I dance or when I teach, because it is what I love, I become very serious,' he admits. 'I told Vick, "As soon as we start rehearsals I will become a different person. I play it straight because I love what I do and I know you have potential." She said, "I can't wait to start."'

GRAZIANO
DI PRIMA

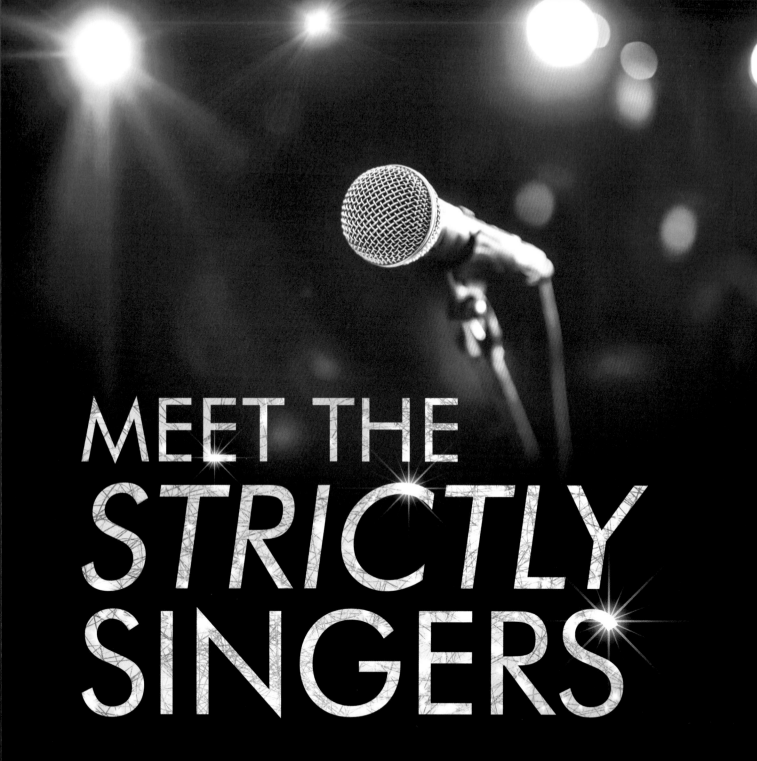

MEET THE *STRICTLY* SINGERS

From Sinatra to Shakira, from Aretha to ABBA, each *Strictly* show features a huge variety of musical styles.

Amazingly, these songs are all sung by four singers whose voices are among the most versatile in the business. Between them, they switch effortlessly from rock to R&B and from swing to soul, and stay pitch-perfect every time.

Tommy Blaize

At nine, Tommy and his brothers Tony and Darrin were already playing the North-West clubs as The Blaize Brothers. After studying at music college and a stint in Spain, Tommy became a session singer and worked with legendary artists including Diana Ross, Queen and Amy Winehouse. As a talented keyboard player, he also toured with the likes of Take That and Robbie Williams.

How do you choose who sings which song?

In a typical week we have around 15 songs. We get the edited versions on Monday, then Musical Director Dave Arch and I listen to them and allocate the singers. They normally jump out at us, because the styles of our voices are so different.

How does it work once you get the tracks?

We all learn our individual parts and then rehearse on a Friday evening and make sure the harmonies are right. Andrea picks up the high harmony, Hayley the middle and Lance and I will work it out between us. We meet in the dressing room an hour before the band rehearsal and go through harmonies to fix anything. If we can't fix it, we wait for Dave and his wonderful ears! All through Saturday we keep tweaking so we're comfortable by showtime.

Favourite artist's songs to sing?

I'm a big fan of Marvin Gaye and Louis Armstrong, so when they come up I'm in my element. But I enjoy singing them all and it's great when I get a style I haven't tried before.

Are there any you just can't sing?

Absolutely loads! But I pass them to someone else. Crazy harmonic stuff, like Queen songs, which are layered up with 30 or 40 vocals, are hard, because there are only four of us. We try to get as close to the edit as we can. It's important we don't improvise, because the couples rehearse all week to that track and we don't want to throw them off.

How do you prepare your voice?

Pineapple is my saviour. It has natural enzymes. If you ever have a cough, don't get cough mixture – eat pineapple. I've tried honey and lemon, and lozenges, and they don't work. Whenever my voice is tired, I have a jar of pineapple next to my microphone.

Hayley Sanderson

As a child, Hayley attended a local theatre group and started singing with her uncle's soul band. After winning a talent contest, she began performing in clubs at the age of 12. She worked with producers Nile Rodgers and Narada Michael Walden before becoming the house singer at Ronnie Scott's Jazz Club and taking part in various recording sessions – where she met Dave Arch.

What is your *Strictly* speciality?

When I first joined it was mostly to cover jazz and softer songs like Eva Cassidy. But it's become more varied and I've done everything from Kate Bush to Katy Perry, opera, rock, musical theatre and traditional Cuban. I don't think there's a genre we haven't covered.

Favourite artist's songs to sing?

Kate Bush, Ella Fitzgerald, Amy Winehouse, Chrissie Hynde and Peggy Lee.

Which songs are the most challenging?

I find Kylie a real challenge as her voice is so far from mine. Some of the famous, unique voices can be impossible. For example, if you're expecting Cher and my voice comes in, it can be a shock to the audience because they are so used to hearing it sung a certain way. We don't impersonate, but we aim for the same style, phrasing and timing as the original vocalist because the dancers choreograph to the words or the singer.

'I have a giant straw and I blow bubbles into water to warm and stretch my vocal cords. It's the perfect exercise for *Strictly* because it's silent . . . You can't make a sound between performances'

Do you have any vocal warm-ups?

Quite a few, but I mostly just do breathing exercises on a Saturday to keep warm in between contestants. I have a giant straw and I blow bubbles into water to warm and stretch my vocal cords. It's the perfect exercise for *Strictly* because it's silent. You can't make a sound between performances, so if I feel my voice has gone cold I can blow into my straw while Claudia is talking to the contestants.

How do you look after your voice in between shows?

Rest and water!

What's the best thing about being part of the *Strictly* team?

Getting to see the routines from the best seat in the house while playing with such an amazing band. There aren't many live bands on TV, especially of that size, and it's an absolute honour to play with them.

Lance Ellington

Lance is the son of band leader Ray Ellington and, as well as having a successful solo career, he has worked with Sting, Michael Jackson, Tina Turner and many more. He also confesses to singing some of 'those really annoying jingles' you've heard on TV ads over the years.

What is your *Strictly* speciality?

Swing and jazz, but I get a variety. There was one show when I did both Meatloaf and Frank Sinatra, going from 'Bat Out of Hell' to 'Come Fly with Me', but that is the beauty of the job.

Which songs are the most challenging?

High rock tracks, like Freddie Mercury, because they're in a much higher key than I would normally sing in. Or songs that are very much of an era, like The Andrews Sisters. It's hard to pick out the way the close harmonies work, but if we're unsure, Dave Arch breaks them down and gives us a vocal part to learn.

What is your most memorable song challenge?

'Gangnam Style' by Psy for Ed Balls. I got the song on the Wednesday and I had two days to learn Korean! It was great fun, though, and one of those standout moments that got played and played.

How do you look after your voice?

I gave up drinking coffee and milk, because dairy products are not great for a vocalist. I don't eat a lot on a *Strictly* day because I like to keep my voice clear. The studio has air conditioning and there are pyrotechnics, which sometimes mean a lot of smoke, so I drink gallons of tea and litres of water to hydrate the voice.

What's the best thing about working on *Strictly*?

It's an exciting show to be part of. There's nothing else like it. It's such a buzz. It's become a huge part of my life and I feel very blessed to be doing something that I love.

Andrea Grant

Andrea studied at the BRIT School before embarking on a singing career. She has toured with the likes of Shirley Bassey, Lisa Stansfield, Robbie Williams and McFly, and joined *Strictly* in series three after getting through open auditions.

What is your *Strictly* speciality?

Big female tunes, like Whitney Houston and Aretha Franklin. Anything soulful. Hayley does the jazzier numbers and we share the pop. If it's rock, Hayley will probably do it, but I have sung those too.

How long do you get to learn the songs?

I start on Monday morning. We have five days to learn between 15 and 20 songs, which is a lot. On Friday, we have an evening rehearsal with the band. On Saturday, we do the show.

How many of the songs will be your lead vocals?

It all depends on what songs the dancers choose, so some weeks I could have six lead vocals and another week just one or two. But we still have all the backing vocals to learn.

How do you emulate so many styles and voices?

Years of practice! As session singers you have to be versatile and we've honed that craft over the years. We've all got pretty good ears.

Favourite artist's songs to sing?

I love singing Whitney Houston songs because she is my idol, but I get very nervous because there is only one Whitney!

Do you have a vocal warm-up?

Not really. There are not enough hours in the day because we start so early on a Saturday.

How do you look after your voice?

Honey, ginger and hot water, and as much vitamin C as possible.

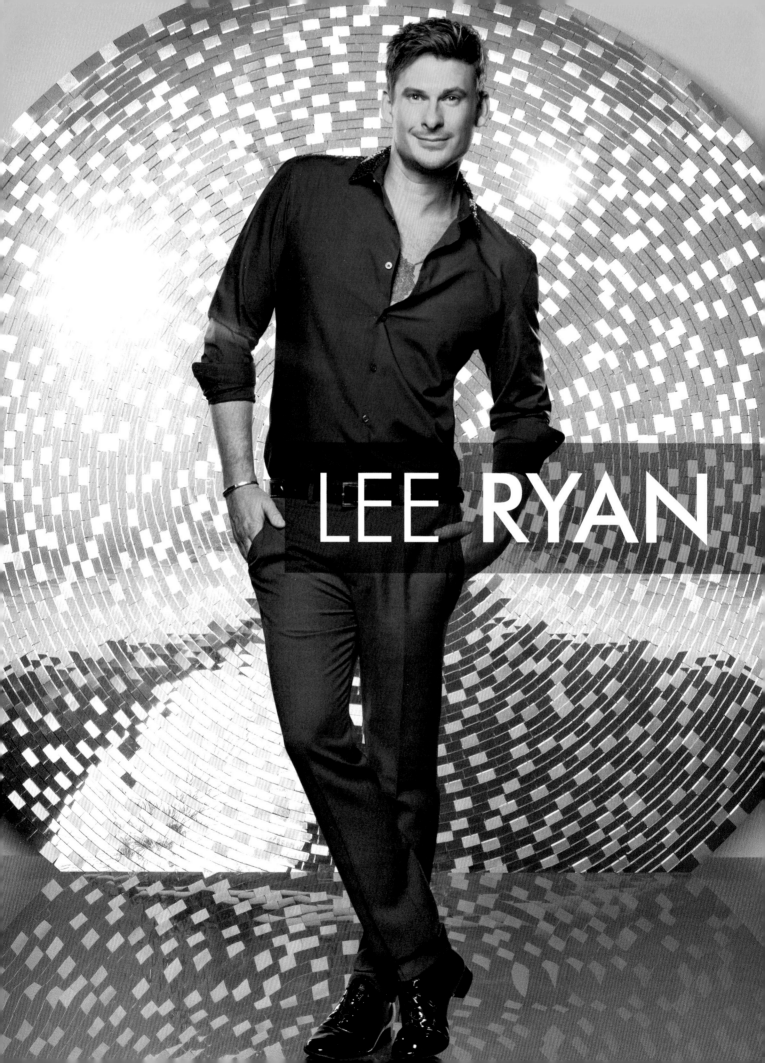

LEE RYAN

The thought of facing the *Strictly* judges doesn't leave Lee Ryan quaking in his boots, because his critics are at home. The dad of two says his 11-year-old daughter Bluebell and nine-year-old son Rayn are not mincing their words.

'When my little girl heard I was doing *Strictly* she said, "Dad, you can't dance"', laughs Lee. 'I asked my son if I am a good dancer, and he said, "No." I said, "You've set me right up. I'm ready for the judges now."'

Lee was born in Chatham, Kent, and shot to fame in the early 2000s as a member of the boy band Blue. The foursome sold 14 million records and scored a string of hits, including 'All Rise' and 'One Love', but split in 2005. Lee had a solo career before branching out into acting. He most recently starred in *EastEnders* as well as touring with the reunited Blue.

Although he has thrown himself into the competition with enthusiasm, the singer admits he had reservations about signing up to *Strictly*.

'I'm really happy that I made the decision to do it,' he says. 'But I was quite nervous at first. It's such a big thing.' When I'm not working, I'm with my kids, so jumping into something like this can be quite daunting. But I'm glad I did.'

Despite his musical background, Lee – who will partner Nadiya Bychkova – insists he has a lot to learn when it comes to dance.

'Have you seen Blue perform?' he says. 'We're like a dad-dance band! "When in doubt, dad it out" is our motto.'

He did seek some words of advice from bandmate Simon Webbe, who appeared on the show in 2014.

'Simon just said, "Enjoy it," and that's the best advice,' says Lee. 'He showed me a few little things and talked about my posture for the Waltz, keeping it upright, but the biggest piece of advice was to be me, to be happy – because I am a happy-go-lucky guy – and to enjoy myself.'

In her first year, Nadiya Bychkova made it to the Quarter-finals with Davood Ghadami and, for her second season, she is hoping the audience and judges will 'All Rise' to give her and dance partner Lee Ryan a standing ovation. But she reveals the Blue singer has a lot to learn, despite dancing on stage in the past.

'Lee is picking up the routine quite well, so I'm happy about that, but he never did ballroom and Latin, so there's a lot of stuff to work out,' Nadiya says. 'It is so different to what he used to do when he was performing with Blue. This is a completely different body position, posture and everything, so we are working on that.

'He is really enjoying it. We are rehearsing from 10 until six, with two breaks, and it's quite full-on. It's quite a shock for the body and it takes a while to get used to it. He's never done this before and now he is doing it for so many hours, so after a few days I could tell he was a bit tired.'

Although his first dance, a Waltz, is as far from a Blue routine as you can get, Nadiya says

he has really taken to ballroom.

'Lee has so much energy and in ballroom we have to keep it calm, but he has worked really hard and he loves the Waltz, the feeling and elegance of it. He keeps telling me he loves how graceful the dance is, so it's great to see he's enjoying it.'

Nadiya was born in Ukraine and moved to Slovenia at 15, where she attended the same dance school as Aljaž Škorjanec. She is a two-time World Champion and European Champion in ballroom and Latin '10' Dance and a multiple-time Slovenian Ballroom and Latin Champion.

The Ukrainian dancer certainly made an impact in her debut series. Taking actor Davood Ghadami all the way to week 11 was no mean feat, considering he had never danced before and he was still doing the day job, filming a big storyline in *EastEnders*.

'Davood is such a nice man,' she says. 'He had no experience with dancing at all.

'He was very dedicated. We would go over and over it again with each routine and only after he thought he had it would he say, "Let's go for a tea break."'

This year, Nadiya is looking forward to not being the new girl any more.

'Last year I didn't really know how it worked, so everything we did was all new to me. I feel more relaxed this year and it's a nice feeling, knowing what to expect and knowing the routine of the season.'

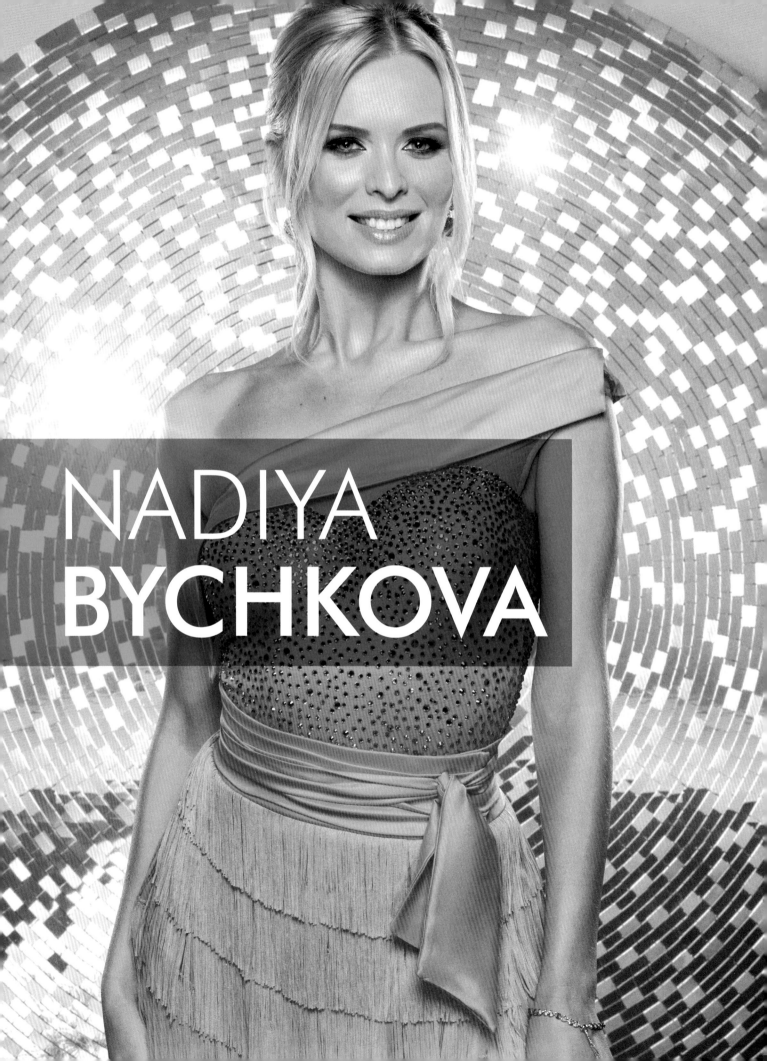

NADIYA
BYCHKOVA

Last year Craig Revel Horwood surprised viewers by bowing at the feet of finalist Debbie McGee. But the acerbic judge says the former magician's assistant deserved every accolade. 'I loved Debbie and I was so pleased she went to the Final,' he explains. 'It was wonderful to see someone older creating such amazing dances. She was incredible, a real inspiration. Her Tango was fantastic, her Argentine Tango was amazing. In fact, every time she stepped onto the dance floor she was brilliant.'

Craig says champion Joe McFadden was a worthy winner, but it was a close-run competition. 'Joe and Katya did a great job and their Viennese Waltz was immaculate, but I would say the four of them – Alexandra Burke, Debbie McGee, Joe McFadden and Gemma Atkinson – all deserved the trophy.'

Craig was equally impressed with new head judge Shirley, who is returning to the panel for her second year.

'I loved Shirley's debut, I thought she was great,' he says. 'She's been a World Champion and she's so knowledgeable, particularly about the Latin. She also gives fantastic advice to the celebrities. I'm happy she's back this year. She's lively, she brings a lot of fun and she brings a really good element to the judging panel.'

What do you think of this year's line-up?

The line-up is brilliant. There are lots of interesting people. Katie Piper is a strong and determined woman. It looks like she is going to be fantastic.

Who else do you have your eye on?

Danny John-Jules has a theatre background and he's got a great personality. It would be great to see an older man bringing some amazing routines to the floor.

Who will surprise us?

We have our second Paralympian, Lauren Steadman, and she's one to watch. I think she's adapting really well and creating new holds to suit her physicality. She's very strong and very fit.

Who will provide the laughs?

Graeme Swann will provide plenty of entertainment, but hopefully he's good as well. He is reminding me a little of Ed Balls in that he will provide comedy, but it seems like he's got good timing.

What is your favourite week?

Musicals Week, because that's my genre, that's what I love and what I've always done for a living. I like the storytelling, I like the music. I am Mister Musical.

CRAIG REVEL HORWOOD

A DAY IN THE LIFE

OF A *STRICTLY* EXEC

For the millions of viewers who tune in every week, *Strictly* is a two-hour treat on a Saturday night with an added dose of sparkle in the Sunday-night results show. But for Executive Producer Louise Rainbow and her team, it means months of planning before the series even begins.

'We start in the spring and our first priority is booking celebrities,' says Louise. 'The Talent Executive and I brainstorm ideas and approach people, then we have casting meetings to firm up the list. We also confirm the professional dancer line-up for the series.

'Next, the Series Editor comes on board and we start planning the content. We meet choreographers, decide on the themed weeks, like the Movies, Musicals and Halloween Specials, work out what we want to do for the red-carpet and launch show and plan the group performances for the entire series.

'As we get closer to the launch show, the pro dancers rehearse the group performances and the team comes on board to plan the VTs (the pre-recorded clips shown before each dance), write the scripts, plan the numbers and work out the scheduling.

'*Strictly* is a real team effort – from the VT team to the live team to the dance team, every person works so hard and contributes so much to the creative vision for the series.'

As soon as the series starts, Louise and many of her team are working seven days a week. But it is Saturday, the day of the live show, when everything finally comes together. Here, Louise talks us through a typical Saturday at the *Strictly* studio in Elstree.

8.30 a.m. I arrive at the studio. We have rehearsals on a Friday and start early on a Saturday.

9 a.m. Dance rehearsals. Every couple runs through their routine three times on Friday, but the orchestra isn't there, so on Saturday morning they run through with the orchestra, which takes the routine to the next level. When you've been rehearsing to a track all week, and then you suddenly rehearse to the live orchestra on Saturday, it's really exciting.

As the couples begin rehearsing, our director and I are in the production gallery, where we can see what is happening on the floor and on camera, and give feedback through the talkback system. By Saturday it's too late to make any major changes, so if we think anything needs changing: the choreography, lighting, graphics on the screens, props or camera coverage, we would need to flag that on a Friday.

10.30 a.m. The professionals rehearse the group routine and, once again, I give my feedback.

11 a.m. The couples' rehearsals continue. While I am watching the rehearsals, I receive the final VT edits to sign off for the show that night. The first edit of the VTs usually come in on a Friday, so when rehearsals finish at 6.30 p.m. on Friday I then view the VTs and feed notes back so that the final VTs can be completed by Saturday morning.

12.30 p.m. Lunch break.

1.30 p.m. Dress rehearsal, when we run the show as a whole. The couples perform their dances in full costume and make-up for the first time, and Tess and Claudia run through their script. Instead of the judges, our runners sit at the judges' desk and give plenty of encouragement to all the couples.

Immediately after the dress rehearsal the heads of department get together and we share notes, because that's the first time we see everything come together with the lighting, the camera coverage, the screens, the props, the costumes, hair and make-up.

In the time available, we can only make minor changes, so if the dress doesn't work with the lighting, it's easier to change the

lighting than the dress. It could be that the hair is down and it would look better up or a make-up tweak. We also give notes on the script to the presenters.

3.30 p.m. The music act for the results show rehearses their number.

4.30 p.m. The celebrities, pro dancers and crew have a dinner break. The audience start arriving at the studio and the excitement and buzz starts to really build.

5.30 p.m. Often the music act for the results show is recorded before the live show.

6.30 p.m. On air!

During the live show I'm in the production gallery (the sound-proofed control room) with Series Editor Sarah James and our Commissioning Editor, Jo Wallace. I'm responsible for all the content and making sure it is appropriate for pre-watershed, and Sarah speaks to Claudia and Tess down the earpiece if we're running over or under and gives notes to the producers on the floor.

8.30 p.m. The live show ends and voting lines open. Between the live show and the results show, which is recorded on Saturday night, we record the group number for the results show. The live team write the script for the results show according to who is in the bottom two.

9.30 p.m. We record the results show.

10.30 p.m. In the last few minutes of recording, I go down onto the studio floor, because I want to be first to commiserate with the couple who didn't go through at the dance-off and also congratulate the couples who have got through. It's so important to be there when people are disappointed, and it's good to talk to each of the couples at the end of the day.

After that, I thank the judges and the presenters.

I leave at around midnight and get home about 1 a.m.

The results show is edited overnight, so I wake up at 8 a.m. on Sunday and start reviewing that and sending my feedback to the editing team. Sarah alternates with me so that neither of us has to work all day every Sunday as well as the other six days a week.

On Monday, the planning begins for the next week's show and I'm also looking back at the Saturday-night show to see if it was as good as it could have been and how can we improve it.

The hours are very long and you could only do it if you absolutely loved it, which I do. It's only from September to Christmas that it's so crazy. The rest of the year I do Monday to Friday, nine to five.

I also have a great team supporting me. Everyone from our make-up team and costume team to the dance team and the lighting team have been working together for years, so we support each other and know how we all work and what is expected.

Plus, I'm working on the best show on TV and on something that the viewers love, so it's exciting and rewarding and I enjoy every minute.

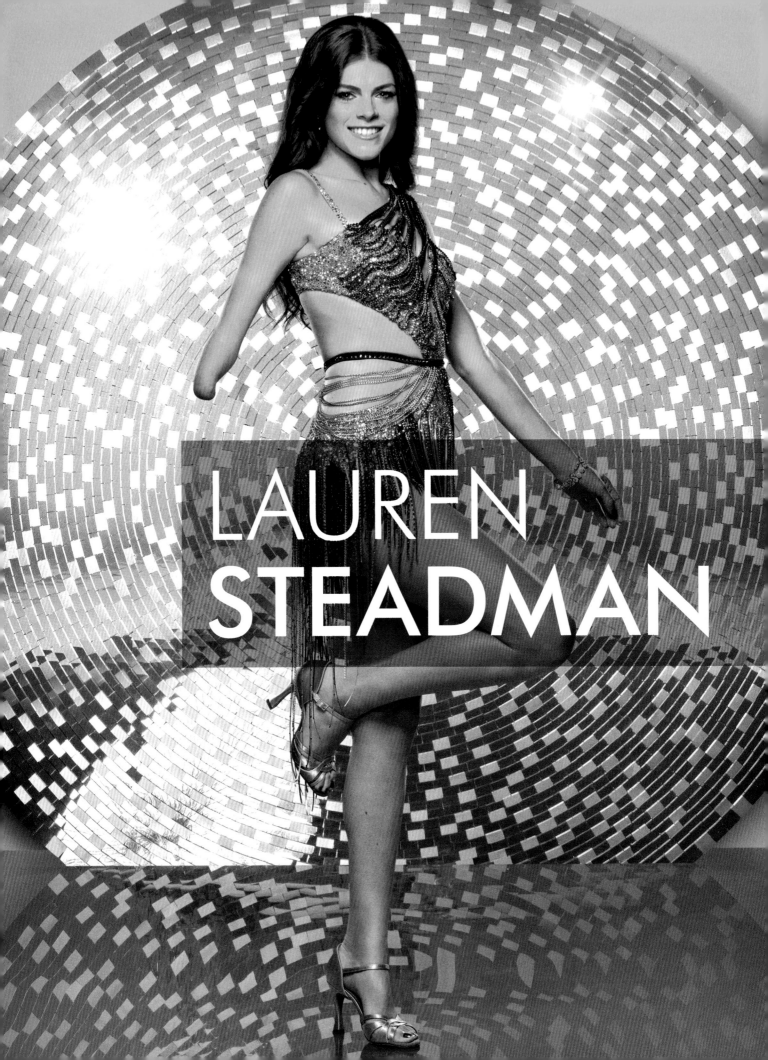

LAUREN
STEADMAN

Lauren Steadman is the second Paralympian to grace the *Strictly* dance floor, after sprinter Jonnie Peacock's star turn last year. Born without a complete right arm, she is a world champion paratriathlete as well as earning silver at the 2016 Paralympics in Rio de Janeiro.

'Jonnie inspired the whole nation with his dance moves,' she says. 'It's a similar thing for me. I want to go out and show that actually it's not disability, it's ability, and inspire people to go outside their comfort zones, learn something new and enjoy themselves. If I can come away with a new skill and something I can do until I'm 80 or 90 then fantastic.'

Lauren was born in Peterborough and started to train as a triathlete in her teens. In 2009 she represented Great Britain in the IPC World Championships in Rio de Janeiro and won gold in the 100-metre relay. In 2014, she won the London World Series Paratriathlon and became the World Champion in Edmonton, Canada, as well as gaining a first-class degree in psychology. She went on to gain a Masters degree in business and management. Then, in 2016, when paratriathlon was introduced as an event in the Rio Paralympics, Lauren took the silver medal, behind US athlete Grace Norman.

Lauren hopes her sporting background will stand her in good stead when it comes to the dance training.

'Being athletes, you fine-tune every single aspect of your life,' she says. 'So it's just another skill that hopefully we can hone in on and go as far as we can.'

However, before she could immerse herself in dance there was the small matter of the World Championships in Australia, which meant she missed a week of training before her first dance.

'My first rehearsal was six days before the first live show, so it's intense, but at the same time I work really well under pressure.'

As her whole life is about speed, Lauren, who is dancing with AJ Pritchard, thinks she'll be better suited to the faster dances, such as the Jive and the Charleston.

'I think I'll find the slow ones harder,' she says. 'The fast stuff is fine, I've got the endurance, but I find it hard to slow down. It's easier when you go faster.'

She acknowledges that the dances in hold might prove difficult but in true Paralympian style, she's up for the challenge.

'I have looked at some of the dances and seen the different styles and I think the biggest challenge will be getting around certain moves with my arm, but that's a challenge I'll take on with AJ. I'm not worried about it. I know we're going to have to think outside the box and perhaps do things differently, but we'll get around it.'

When Paralympian Lauren Steadman was paired with AJ Pritchard on the launch show, she was so excited she jumped into his arms – and took him by surprise.

AJ, who partnered Olympic gymnast Claudia Fragapane on his 2016 *Strictly* debut, had another surprise. He would only have three hours training before Lauren jetted off to Australia for the World Championships and only two days after her return.

'Having another athlete, and one whose story is so inspirational, is amazing,' he says. 'In the three hours we had, every second was valuable and we were both so focused. It wasn't a messing-around-and-having-fun training session. We pretty much got everything done in three hours, so I was extremely happy.

'It's great to have someone who wants to learn and put the hard work in. That's all I can ever ask for as a teacher.'

Although Lauren's triathlon career means she is incredibly fit, AJ introduced her to muscles she didn't know she had.

'The day after the training session she got on the plane and told me, "I am in agony. I can feel my neck, my back, my feet …" I said, "We only did three hours. Imagine how you'd feel if you did 12 hours!" That's what we will be trying to do.

'Running, cycling and swimming are very linear, so it's very direct strength. But when you are dancing you are doing lots of rotation and you might use one side of the body more than the other. You are not in natural positions, so it does make your body think.'

Born in Stoke-on-Trent, AJ learned to dance at his parents' dance school and in 2015 he became British Open Youth Latin Champion and European Youth Latin Champion. He was National Youth Latin Champion for three years in a row from 2012–2014.

This will be his third year on *Strictly* and AJ is excited to be partnered with Lauren, who was born without a complete right arm.

'When we first started dancing in hold, it felt completely comfortable, which is exactly what both of us want to portray – that there is no disadvantage.

'Lifts might be the only things that work differently as I have to readjust where I place my weight. As a choreographer, I'm very excited to try new things that maybe I wouldn't have tried before.'

Last year, AJ reached the Semi-final with singer Mollie King and says he had a 'fantastic year'.

'The more hours and the more hard work Mollie could put in, the more relaxed she was on the night. I think Lauren will want to work just as hard, so I can't wait.'

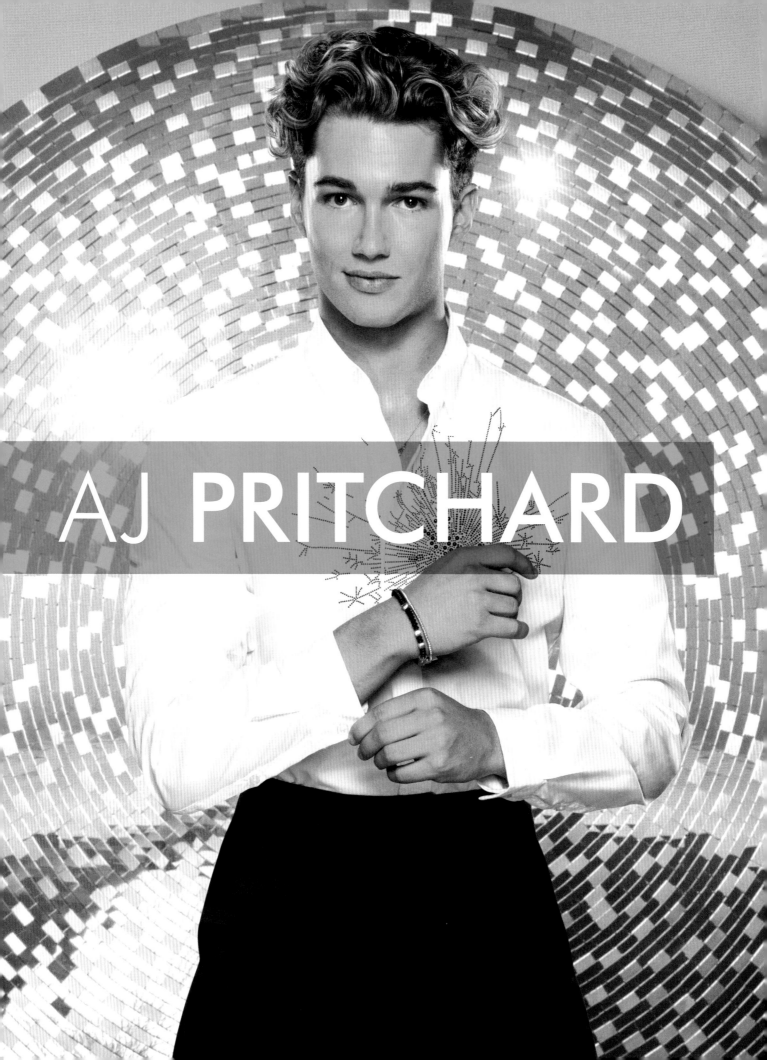
AJ PRITCHARD

BALLROOM
BINGO

Missing a night at the bingo to watch your favourite Saturday-night show? Never fear, Ballroom Bingo is here! Suitable for one to four players, our fun game combines the thrill of the bingo hall with everything *Strictly*. All you have to do is pick a card and mark off the events as they occur in the show. But make sure you use pencil, so you can keep playing every week.
Eyes down for a full house!

BINGO

Darcey gives a 9	A chair is used as a prop
Craig awards a 2	Judges award a total score of 23
Craig says 'A-ma-zing'	Bruno compares a celebrity to an animal

BINGO

Shirley gives a 10	Bruno jumps out of his chair
Craig says 'Dull'	Judges award a total score of 25
A table is used as a prop	Darcey says 'I loved it'

BINGO

Craig dusts off his 10 paddle	Craig says 'Dis-ast-er'
Shirley moves to avoid Bruno's expressive arms	Judges award a total score of 34
A celebrity flies in	One of the judges mentions 'hip action'

BINGO

Bruno gives a 9	Craig says 'Fab-u-lous'
A dance begins on the stairs	Judges award a total score of 19
Shirley demonstrates a dance move with her arms	A judge mentions 'heel leads'

Presenter Tess Daly has been sizing up the new recruits and she likes what she sees. This year's intakes, she says, have a whole lot of energy. 'As a collective, they seem to bounce off each other,' she says. 'The energy is contagious. Lots of personalities shone through on the launch show.

'Stacey Dooley was a laugh a minute. She was entertaining everyone backstage with what we've already christened "the Dooley Drop". If she pulls that one out on a live show, mouths will be on the floor. It's extraordinary.

'Charles Venn is charming everybody with his personality. Susannah Constantine is hysterical. Without a doubt, she'll keep Anton on his toes.

'Faye Tozer is a massive *Strictly* fan. When Steps performed on the show she insisted on having her photo taken in the judges' seats – every single one. She's so excited at being on the show she cried for a full 20 minutes when she got the call.

'Graeme Swann is a really likeable chap. He's going round slapping everyone's back, tons of camaraderie. He and Oti are definitely ones to watch. He said his kids are delighted because they watch the show every week. He wants to be Superman for his kids.

'Seann Walsh's major concern was missing Queens Park Rangers matches on Saturdays, so we made him a sequinned QPR scarf and I've never seen anyone so happy.

'Prior to the launch show the celebs and pros meet and spend two days in an intensive dance workshop while the pro dancers teach them the group dance so by the time we get to the launch they have a good idea of the styles of each pro. It's great to watch their reaction when they get paired up and see how thrilled they are.

'We've got some fantastic pairings. Vick Hope and Graziano are a fantastic couple. They will be dynamite.

'Lauren threw herself so enthusiastically into AJ's arms that he almost dropped her!'

Tess has high hopes for world champion paratriathlete, Lauren. 'She loves to dance and sees it as a relaxing pastime compared to her day job. Good luck keeping up with her, AJ!'

Tess may have 15 series under her belt, but she's still bowled over by a breathtaking dance.

'Last year, Alexandra Burke did a jive to "Proud Mary" and the energy in the studio was amazing,' she says. 'Her ability and passion just shone through. It was almost an out-of-body experience and I loved it. Joe McFadden, Debbie McGee and Gemma Atkinson were also incredible performers and had brilliant routines.'

Last year's *Strictly* was the most watched yet and Tess says it was one of the closest Finals to date. 'It was too close to call. I love it when that happens and it's down to the last few votes and the showdance. Who will pull it out of the bag? It makes the Final even more exciting.

'I think this year could be just as unpredictable. Bring it on.'

TESS DALY

DR RANJ SINGH

Having passed his first GCSE at the age of eight, Dr Ranj Singh is obviously quick to learn. But he's not sure if his head will be able to tell his feet what they need to know.

'I am a geek,' he says. 'I like to study and study things until I get it right and I'm hoping that attention to detail in learning will help me pick stuff up. But what I've discovered is that learning movement is totally different to learning information, so I don't know what it's going to be like, I really don't.'

Born in Kent, Ranj studied medicine in London and became an NHS clinician. In 2012, he created and presented the award-winning children's TV show *Get Well Soon* and went on to become a resident doctor on ITV's *This Morning*. He has also presented *Save Money: Good Health* and written two children's books, while still working for the NHS.

Ranj, who is paired with Janette Manrara, describes himself as a 'social dancer'.

'My friends would describe me as a dad dancer,' he admits. 'I do like to dance, but I do it for fun.'

As a ballroom novice, Ranj is excited to be taking on the different dances but admits there are some that he is keener on.

'I'm looking forward to the Paso Doble because it's dramatic and there's a story and it's all very sexy,' he says. 'It's not an experience that I'm used to. But I'm worried about the Charleston, because it is fast and there's many legs going everywhere, and the Argentine Tango, where they do all the kicks. I'd be scared I'd kick Janette in the shins.'

Making new friends and spending time with them has proved to be an added bonus for Dr Ranj, who says the celebrities and dancers bonded immediately.

'We only spent three or four days together in group rehearsal and because we're all in a very similar situation – we're all panicking about learning routines, getting moves right – it felt like the first day of school. Everyone's nervous so we all bonded, because that's what happens when you're faced with a challenge with a bunch of people. We're all helping each other out. There is no competition.

'It sounds like a cliché, but it very much feels like a family. I'm starting to miss the group when I'm away, which is a great place to be.'

The good doctor follows in the footsteps of *This Morning* presenter Ruth Langsford and she had some words of advice for him.

'She said, "Just enjoy it. It will be a rollercoaster and there will be times when you feel like you can't do it and there will be times when you are flying. But this will never happen again,"' he says. 'You don't do *Strictly* twice, and you've got to make the most of it.'

Having been paired up with TV medic Dr Ranj Singh, Janette Manrara is prescribing plenty of hard work and lots of fun. 'I was over the moon to get Ranj,' she says. 'This is the first year that I have had no idea who I was going to get. Because of my height, there are normally only one or two I could be paired with, but this year I had a few options so I was really nervous.

'They were all amazing in different ways, but when I got Ranj I was ecstatic because I had met him before and I knew how lovely he was. I feel like we are the perfect fit for each other. We are the Pocket Rockets. We're really small, but we have *big* personalities.'

As Dr Ranj is still committed to hospital work and regular appearances on *This Morning*, the couple are rehearsing every evening until 10 p.m. But Janette says her new pupil is 'really keen and excited'.

'He has loads of potential, but there's a lot of work to do,' she says. 'It's exciting for me to have someone to work with that can get better and improve week in and week out, and that people can actually see a proper journey with.'

Whatever his dance skills, Dr Ranj is certainly committed to being *Strictlified*.

'On the first day of rehearsals Ranj showed up in black trackies, which looked very normal until he turned to the side. They had a huge strip of rainbow glitter sparkles going down the leg! He said, "Perfect for my first day of *Strictly* rehearsals, don't you think?"

'This is going to be the most fun season in that sense, because he is ready to throw on all the glitter, all the sparkles, he's ready to dance, to sweat and to do whatever it takes. His energy is so exciting.'

Janette was born in Miami, Florida. She was a principal dancer in the TV series and live tour of *Glee*, and performed with Jennifer Lopez at the 82nd Academy Awards. She was also a finalist in *So You Think You Can Dance* in the US. She joined *Strictly* in 2013 and last year she partnered Aston Merrygold.

Looking forward to the next series, Janette says the launch show has set the scene for a spectacular season.

'There were so many things in the launch show that I'm excited about,' she says. 'Being a Cuban, I loved the group number to "Havana", with the introduction of the three new pros. I felt like I was back with my family in Miami, dancing at the best party ever. The launch show was a good teaser for what is to come this season.'

JANETTE
MANRARA

COUPLE'S
CHOICE

Back in 2009, *Strictly* introduced the Charleston, and the Roaring Twenties favourite has been a roaring success ever since. But the other dances have stayed the same – until now.

In this series, celebrities and pro dancers will get a chance to showcase some very different skills in a fresh dance category: the Couple's Choice. As the weeks progress, the couples will get the chance to try their hand (and feet) at three modern styles. And the beauty of all three is that there are no rules, which means unlimited lifts and tricks.

The three styles are:

- ♥ Contemporary – taking inspiration from ballet, lyrical and modern dance.

- ♥ Street/commercial – all styles of urban dance and commercial pop. From hip hop to music videos.

- ♥ Theatre/jazz – think musical theatre, including elements of tap, soft shoe, burlesque and jazz.

The new styles will give the pros free rein to be as creative as they like, as Tess Daly explains.

'There are no specific rules,' she says. 'So I love the idea of the Couple's Choice. It will be more freestyle, and they are new disciplines for us because we have never done street or contemporary. Yes, we have Musicals Week, but this is a whole new interpretation, so it's very exciting.'

The Judges' Verdicts

Will the new freestyle dance get a perfect 10 from the judges?

Shirley Ballas

'Everything has its time and I think any form of dance that is added is great. We're used to seeing the six ballroom, five Latin and also the Argentine Tango, the Charleston and the Salsa, but I think this will be a really different challenge. It's a fantastic idea.'

Craig Revel Horwood

'I'm looking forward to the new dances this year. Seeing some contemporary, jazz and musical theatre coming into the show is a real boost. We could see soft-shoe shuffles, some tap, plus they'll be allowed to do as many lifts as they like, which currently only happens in the showdance in the Final. It gives them a bit more freedom and artistic expression and the opportunity to tell the story.'

Bruno Tonioli

'Couple's Choice is very exciting. They can choose a new style and that will be really interesting. We have done contemporary and jazz on *Dancing with the Stars* in America for years and it always works really well.'

Darcey Bussell

'I'm really excited about the Couple's Choice. I think it will be a great addition for the pros and they can be a bit more experimental. That will also help the celebrities, because we have so many set dances and they are all being compared with each other, so this will allow them to show different strengths. Even though there are techniques that come with the contemporary and commercial and jazz, they are freer. It will give that more theatrical and emotional side. I come from the theatre world, rather than the competitive world, so I love the idea. It will be fun.'

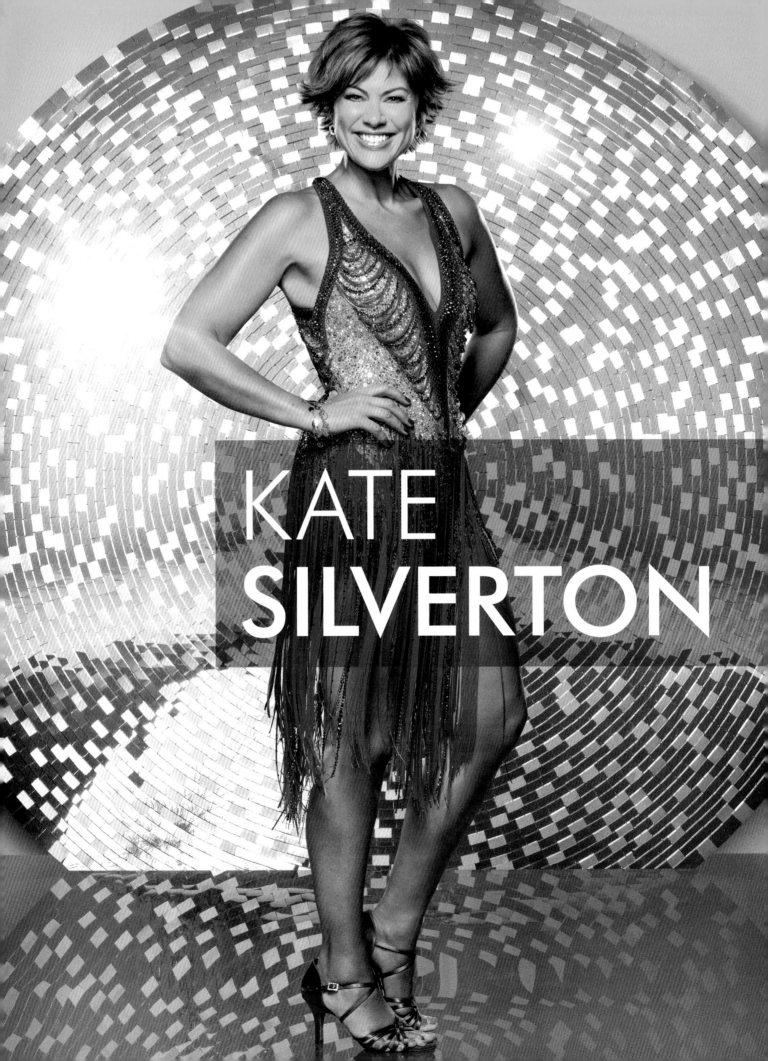

KATE
SILVERTON

Newsreader Kate Silverton will have two avid fans watching at home when she takes to the dance floor. Daughter Clemency, seven, and four-year-old son Wilbur can't wait to see Mum strutting her stuff.

'My little girl is really starting to get into it, which is lovely,' she says. 'It's a really nice bonding thing, talking about all the sparkles and everything. My little boy is only four and a little bemused by it all.'

Born in Essex, Kate took a degree in psychology at Durham University before training as a journalist at the BBC. She got her first presenting job on Tyne Tees Television, but she soon returned to the BBC as a reporter and, later, a news anchor. She is now a regular presenter on *BBC News* at one, six and ten as well as the weekend bulletins.

Kate, who is partnered by Aljaž Škorjanec, has been keen to take to the *Strictly* floor for years, but says the time is now right.

'I've always loved it as a viewer, but you have no idea what is involved until you get into it,'

she says. 'I was asked a fair number of years ago and I was going off to Iraq and then I was going off to Afghanistan. Then I was pregnant and raising my babies. But now it just feels that it is absolutely the right time. Physically, though, I probably should have done this 12 years ago!

'My children are able to enjoy it now, plus they will both be at school, so I can drop them off, do the training and then do the pick-up. Perhaps I can take Aljaž with me!'

Although she was athletic as a child, competing in swimming and triathlon, Kate is a dance novice and confesses to knowing very little about ballroom and Latin.

'Basically, my brain just says, "That's a slow dance and that's a fast dance." That's it. But I've always wanted to do the Tango, the sexy one, where you flick your legs. I know it's a really hard one and I'll probably end up kicking someone, but to be able to do that well would be amazing.'

As a newsreader, Kate is friends with plenty of *Strictly* alumni, including Katie Derham, Naga Munchetty and Charlotte Hawkins.

'Katie Derham told me it will be like nothing else I have ever done and described it as being "a rhinestoned blitz spirit with everyone pulling together through an extraordinary (and glittery) few weeks and months".'

After reaching last year's Final with Gemma Atkinson, Aljaž Škorjanec is hoping to make headlines with newsreader Kate Silverton. 'It's great that we are starting from scratch,' he explains. 'It gives me the opportunity to teach someone from the very beginning, which is always very rewarding. The progress we see from day one in rehearsals to the day they actually get on that floor in the live show is huge.

'Kate is doing really well. She's picking up steps quickly, but it is a learning curve for her and for me. The first few days are really interesting, because I am getting to know her, learning the best way to teach her, seeing what her strengths are, what comes naturally and what we have to work on.

'She has an incredible amount of sass and charisma and a lot of talent. She is very enthusiastic, and she seems like she is loving it so far. I am going to make sure that she loves every single second of the competition.'

Aljaž took up dancing at the age of five and won 19 championships in ballroom and Latin in Slovenia, representing his country in the World Championships for over a decade. Aljaž joined *Strictly* in 2013 and he lifted the glitterball with Abbey Clancy in his first year.

Last year was his second appearance in the Final and he says he had a ball with Gemma.

'More than anything, I was extremely proud of Gemma. Like Kate, she had never danced before she did *Strictly*, so I was teaching someone from the very beginning to get her all the way to the Final. I was very proud of her and myself and very proud we achieved that.

'I was thrilled to get her to the Final and she performed brilliantly. It was really rewarding for me to be next to her. We became really great friends.'

As he prepares for the next series, Aljaž is still buzzing from the launch show.

'It was the best launch show we have ever done,' he says. 'Dancing the opening number with Chic and Nile Rodgers, who are legends, was absolutely incredible. We always have wonderful launch shows. It was a bit of a new look this year and it set up the tone for the whole season very nicely. We set the bar really high and we'll be raising it as the series goes on.'

ALJAŽ ŠKORJANEC

Last year Shirley Ballas took on the role of head judge for the first time and seamlessly slotted into the judging panel. But she admits that her first show left her trembling with nerves.

'The contestants thought they were nervous – I was more nervous than all of them put together!' she laughs. 'So I can sympathise with the celebrities. When you are coming down those stairs and you have millions of viewers looking at you, and you don't know whether the country is going to take to you, that's more nerve-wracking than any World Championship I've ever won.'

Even so, Shirley says she enjoyed every minute of her debut series.

'It took me a while to get used to everything,' she admits. 'You're going live so you can't afford to put a foot wrong.'

'I enjoyed the competitors' journey and seeing what the professionals came up with every week,' Shirley says. 'I'm truly grateful to be doing a second series, because now I feel I can relax a little and I know the ropes, so I can't wait.'

Did you enjoy the launch show?

It was spectacular. The atmosphere was electric. Backstage the contestants are all nervous and the professionals are ready to take on the world for the next three months. It's great because we can stand back and see them all full of energy and ready to go.

What do you think of the line-up?

There are some talented people on the show, some funny people and it's a diverse group. It's an enigma to me who could run away with the glitterball trophy because it looks like it's going to be a close-run race. So stay tuned.

Do you have your eye on anyone already?

I spotted a few people in the group dance that looked like they may be pretty impressive. There is so much going on in the group dance. There are 15 contestants, all the pros and they are changing partners and they have to remember where to dance to. Normally, people make mistakes left, right and centre, but everybody did really well.

Do you think you'll be less nervous this time?

I always put pressure on myself. I want to do an amazing job for the celebrities, so that they can improve week by week, and for the viewer at home. So, yes, I always have butterflies in my tummy.

Favourite moment of the last series?

I would have to say when the Reverend Richard Coles came down on a cloud. I wasn't expecting it at all. That lovely man in his collar descending from the sky will stick with me till I pop my clogs.

SHIRLEY BALLAS

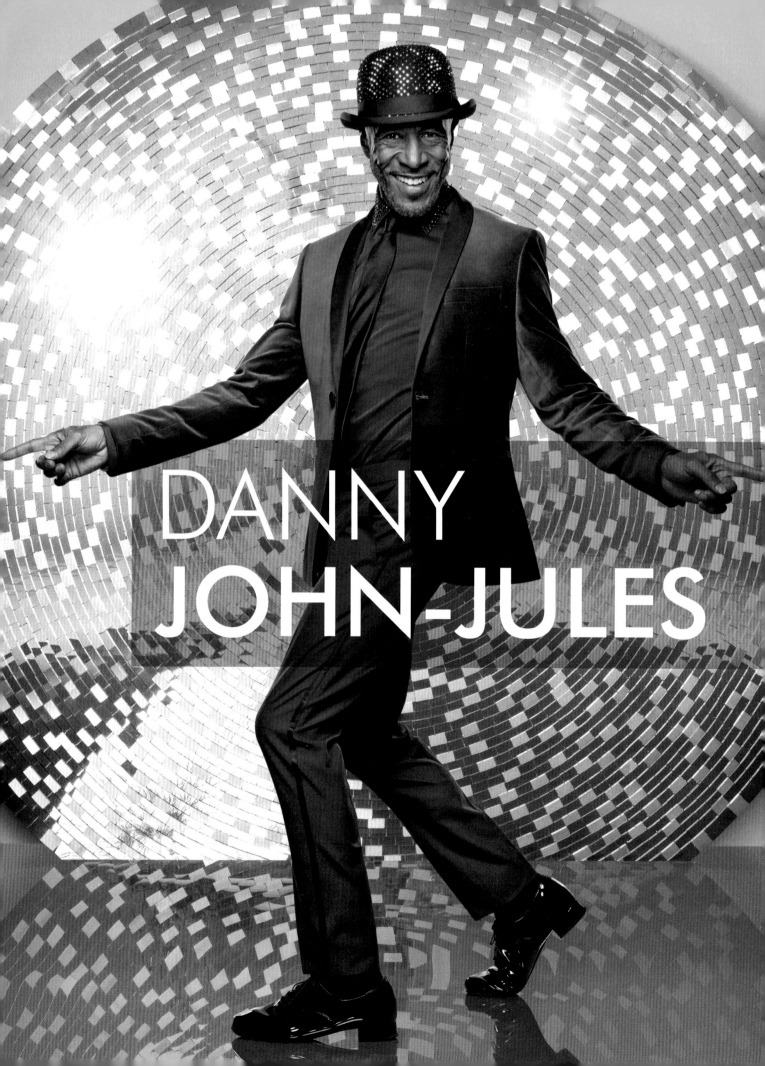

DANNY
JOHN-JULES

After years of playing Cat in *Red Dwarf*, Danny John-Jules is used to flamboyant clothing and statement styles, so being *Strictlified* is not a problem.

'It's a bit like my career has been in the past, really – dressing up, spangly clothes, diamantés, big earrings and more make-up than Tina Turner,' he jokes.

The London-born actor started his career in musical theatre, starring in the original West End production of *Starlight Express*. Four years later he auditioned to play Cat in the BBC's sci-fi comedy series *Red Dwarf*, turning up half an hour late dressed in his grandad's zoot suit, and promptly landed the role. He has since starred in 11 series of the show, as well as playing Officer Dwayne Myers in BBC drama *Death in Paradise*.

Although he started in musical theatre, Danny, who is partnered by Amy Dowden, hasn't been in a show for over 20 years and he says *Strictly* is like going back to his roots.

'I thought that my musical theatre career was pretty much over,' he says. But *Strictly* is probably the closest I'm ever going to get to doing anything musical-theatre-like again – with the spangles, sparkles and jazz hands.'

'I've seen all of the others dancing and thought, "Wow, this is really good." People are going to be surprised.'

However, he believes decades in the acting business have prepared him for any constructive criticism he might get from the judges.

'People ask me how I feel about being judged, but that happens every time I go to an audition,' he says. 'That's what you have to do. You are there to be judged. Even when you've got the gig, you go on stage and perform it, you get judged again by the critics. So for me, it's like, "Bring it on!" I don't mind being judged.'

Dad-of-two Danny says his family are *Strictly* fans and can't wait to see him strut his stuff on the dance floor.

'My other half was the first person I told and she was loving it,' he says. 'We watch it with the kids, so they're all over the moon.'

Amy Dowden's second year on *Strictly* sees her dancing with Danny John-Jules, and she thinks the *Red Dwarf* star could be out of this world. 'I was really happy to get Danny because he's got an amazing work ethic, which I could see from the two training days we had with the celebrities before the launch show,' she says. 'He was constantly practising. With this competition, hard work always pays off. Also, he's lovely and bubbly.'

The actor has a background in musical theatre, but, as Amy explains, that is not always an advantage.

'Although it is great for stamina and performance skills, technically, in the fundamentals of ballroom and Latin, it's going to be harder.' Her new pupil is a quick learner, though.

'He learned the entire routine in one day, but that's just the steps,' she says. 'After learning that we have to put it to music, get the frame, the technique. He has to learn the steps first before I start teaching about his head, his arms, his footwork. You can't think about a million things at once. But he's doing great. He's so positive, he has so much energy. I have to tell him to have a water break, because he's just go, go, go.'

Amy was born and bred in Caerphilly, South Wales, and began dancing at the age of eight. She was the 2017 British National Champion and is one of the highest-ranking ballroom and Latin professional dancers in the UK. When Amy joined *Strictly* last year she danced with Brian Conley, going out in week five.

'I had the perfect first year,' she says. 'Everybody made me feel so welcome. Brian and I had a great time.

'I was lucky enough to go on and win Children in Need, with Mark Curry, and I danced in the Christmas Special with Colin Jackson, so it was a great year.'

Oddly, it was not the first time Amy had met Colin through ballroom dancing.

'Ten years almost to the day before we danced together, Colin presented a documentary that featured me and my dance partner. They filmed me leading up to the Welsh Championships and he remembered because he had come to my school, watched me train and come to the competition. Isn't that mad? Ten years later I was dancing with him.'

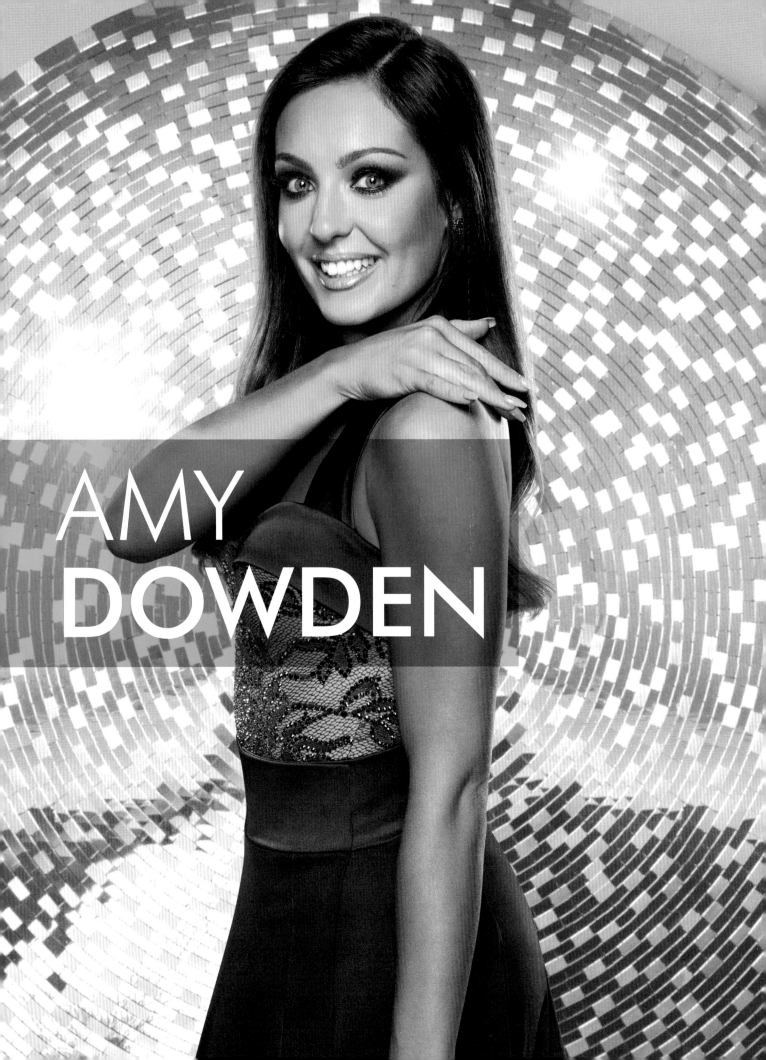

AMY
DOWDEN

FROM DRAWING BOARD TO
DANCE FLOOR

How a *Strictly* routine comes together

By the time the couples stride down the famous stairway on Saturday night, their routines have been memorised, polished and (hopefully) perfected.

But behind each *Strictly* dance lies days and weeks of planning by all the teams, from costume, hair and make-up to props, choreography and lighting. Here, the show's Creative Director of Choreography Jason Gilkison and Series Editor Sarah James reveal what it takes to put a routine together, from day one.

Before the series

In the run-up to the series, Louise Rainbow – the Executive Producer – and the production teams meet to plan the early dances and from then on

they will work two or three weeks in advance.

'Before we decide on the early dances we like to get to know the celebrities,' says Sarah. 'We have group discussions about routines and work out a good balance of dances to make the show as entertaining as possible.'

'We try not to use a music track that has been danced to in the last couple of years and we try to maintain variety,' explains Sarah. 'Also, if there has been a huge hit recently, we'll look to include that, too.'

Three weeks in advance

As soon as the couples are paired, the pros have meetings with the production team including Executive Producer Louise Rainbow, the Dance Producer Jack Gledhill, Jason and the rest of the team to plan their first dances.

'The pros are provided with the edits of their music choices and talk about the routines,' explains Sarah. 'They often come up with their own ideas or, often for the first dances, we give them a concept tailored to the celebrity's job or name – like "Good Golly, Miss Molly" for Mollie King's first dance and the Reverend Richard Coles coming down on a cloud to "There Must Be an Angel Playing With My Heart".'

The couples then have two weeks to put together their first routines and get to know the dance styles that best suit the celebrities. During that time, Jason and his two assistants – Trent and Ash-leigh – spend a couple of hours with each couple.

'I am a sounding board for the pros,' explains Jason. 'Creatively, it helps to bounce ideas off each other and we help them with research for something exciting they want to try because the pros have so much to do, with group numbers and teaching the celebs.' Once the dances and musical tracks have

been confirmed, the professionals come up with the theme, and take their ideas to the producers.

'It's a collaboration, but whatever is chosen, we try to make it work,' says Sarah. 'Once we get their suggestions, there's a meeting with Lousie Rainbow, the dance team including Jason and Jack, myself, the set designer, graphics, lighting etc., and we work out the details. The costume team, led by Vicky Gill, will also liaise separately with the pro and celebrity on the look.' Props and stage builds are agreed a few weeks in advance as many are made from scratch and timing is a big consideration.

'Another consideration for props,' explains Sarah, 'is that the floor team only have 90 seconds to set the props in place, so we have to keep that in mind.'

'Discussions start early on with production designer Catherine Land, who will either design and build things or hire them.' The teams then produce a concept document detailing the various aspects of the routine, including colour schemes, props and special

Debbie's showdance concept document

effects, the backdrop that will be projected on the screens and even the starting position of the dance. The concept or storyline is explained at the start and to illustrate the look, mood boards are compiled using relevant pictures and inspirations. For instance, Debbie McGee's showdance document included pictures of music boxes and a ballerina dressed in grey chiffon, signalling the look.

'The concept document is crucial for inspiration,' says Sarah. 'We have a meeting with costume early on in the week to make sure there is a good mix of different colours among the couple numbers. Make-up only come in on Saturday, but our supervisor, Lisa Armstrong, will be looking at the concept document and talking to costume throughout the week.'

The week of the show: Sunday

'There isn't much free time in the week, so Sunday is a crucial time for the pros to get their steps out of their heads and move on to the next routine.

At the same time Louise, Jason, Sarah, Jack and the rest of the teams are rejigging plans for the following week, based on the dance-off result.

'We never know who is going to be eliminated, so sometimes we end up with too many ballroom numbers, for example, and we might have to do a shuffle around,' says Jason. 'Or we've built a big prop for someone and they're eliminated, so we work out if we can use it for another dance.'

Monday to Thursday

By the beginning of the week the theme and the music are locked down and the professionals are working on the steps.

'I encourage the pros to get the framework of the routine down as early in the week as possible and write down the parts they're not sure about, then chat to me,' says Jason. 'Then we can bounce off their choices to fill those gaps.

'The professionals have to be flexible. If the celebrity can't get that lift that they had in mind, they may have to drop it.'

The couples have four days of training in their individual studios before taking it to Elstree Studios to try it on the *Strictly* dance floor.

'From Monday to Thursday we ask for a minimum of 12 hours' rehearsal, although a lot of them do a lot more.'

'From Monday to Thursday we ask for a minimum of 12 hours' rehearsal, although a lot do more,' explains Sarah. 'We encourage them not to do too much, because that can cause injuries, but most do way over the minimum. Again, Jason and his assistants are there to help.

'The couples get a visit every week, either from myself or one of my assistants, to check that everything is going well.

'The pros all use our visits differently. They might use the Choreography Assistant to show their celebrity how a section of the routine looks and help the celebrity understand the step better. Or sometimes, we'll spend an hour working out choreography ideas with the pros while the celebrity takes a break.

'The important thing is that it is their decision and everything the pro decides to do has to come from their heads.'

Jason's team will also point out any infringements of the dance rules. 'If there is an illegal lift involved, or the beginning is too long, I'll point it out and then it's the pro's decision if they choose to leave it in.' For every pro the stage in the week when they have nailed down their final routine varies.

'They all have a different process,' Jason says. 'Some pros tend to get their routines down quickly, on the first day, whereas others will try out different steps, so the first few days are more experimental.'

Throughout the week the couples are also liaising with costume. Vicky Gill and her team aim to get all the dresses and suits to Elstree Studios by Thursday night, ready for fittings on Friday.

For Louise Rainbow and the full production teams there is a final planning meeting on Thursday, ahead of the rehearsals. 'We talk about the Saturday coming up and the following Saturday, so working two weeks in advance. We talk about the routines with the director, graphics, lighting, props, set design, etc., so we are all on the same page,' says Sarah. 'Any last-minute concerns can be raised, as well as laying the ground for the next routines.'

Friday
By Friday's studio rehearsals, all the elements of the dance have come together and the couples perform the dance for the first time in the *Strictly* studio.

'If anything is not right or the pro isn't

happy with something, we can still tweak,' says Sarah. 'But we can't make major changes at that stage.'

Each couple rehearses the routine three times without the band, dancing to the recorded track they use in practice. Throughout the day, the couples are in and out of wardrobe for final fittings and to discuss any added embellishments ahead of Saturday's dress run.

Saturday
The big day.

The couples rehearse with the live orchestra before the dress run, when everyone performs in full costume and make-up for the first time.

'The last 24 hours into the show is crucial,' says Jason. 'That's when we have to make sure everything is spot on. By the dress run

everything has come together. If anything needs sorting it's up to the wire.

'The costume, hair and make-up departments are amazing. There's more choreography going on there than on the dance floor sometimes!

'I look at people half an hour before the show and think, "How are you going to be ready on time?" but somehow everybody makes it down those stairs and looks wonderful.'

By the time the nation tunes in on Saturday night, every tiny wrinkle has been ironed out.

'Once we are on air there's a feeling of calm for me,' Jason says. 'The nerves are crackling and it's exciting, but I am confident the dances will go well. A lot of hard work goes into the show, but it's such a well-oiled machine. It's a pleasure to be part of it.'

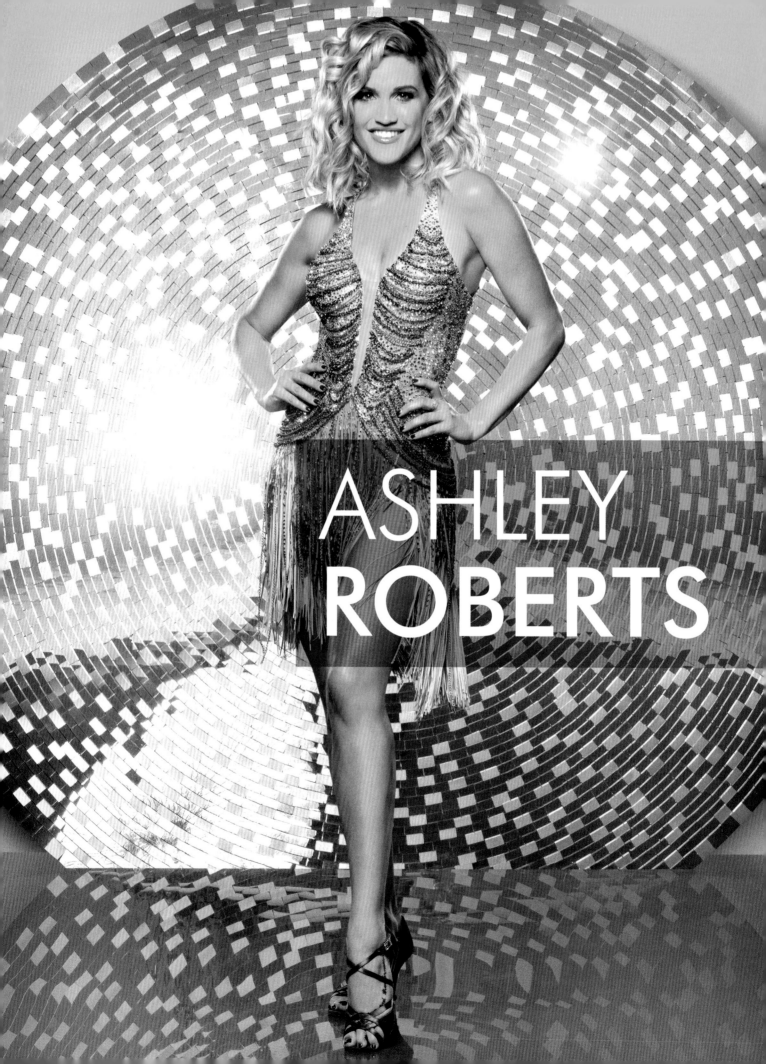

ASHLEY
ROBERTS

For Ashley Roberts, appearing on *Strictly Come Dancing* is a dream come true. 'It's such an amazing show with an amazing audience,' she says. 'You get to learn a skill. There's camaraderie. We get glammed up in fun outfits. I feel like it's a heartfelt show. It feels good for the soul.'

Ashley was born in Phoenix, Arizona, but moved to Los Angeles at 19 to pursue a career as a performer. Within six months she had joined The Pussycat Dolls, who were being moulded into a mainstream pop group. They went on to release two albums and scored global hits with such singles as 'Don't Cha' and 'Stickwitu' before Ashley left, after seven years, in 2010. She went on to have a brief solo career before appearing in *I'm a Celebrity … Get Me Out of Here!* and judging on two series of *Dancing on Ice*.

Although she danced with The Pussycat Dolls, Ashley says the *Strictly* routines will still be a challenge.

'I do have rhythm, which is always a bonus, and I think I'll be able to pick it up well,' she says. 'But it's just really understanding the weight and the movement and the style. Having the guy lead is just foreign to me because we did choreographed pieces and what I've done with the Dolls is very different to doing a Tango!'

She admits that her previous performance experience means the audience will be 'setting the bar high' in their expectations.

'I have performed in my past, but it is a new skill, so I'm really excited to learn the ballroom and the Latin and to hopefully perform in the way it's meant to be done,' she says. 'That is something I am going to have to focus on and learn how to do, which I am excited about. I'm so grateful to be here and I really want to learn and get out there and perform.'

The American singer, who is paired with Pasha Kovalev, is looking forward to a 'little sassy Tango' but admits she's 'scared' of ballroom.

However, she's happy to face the judges and promises to listen to everything she's told.

'I think I'm more nervous about getting the first number out of the way,' she says. 'The judges have to go in and they have to give opinions on what they see, because that's their job. I definitely want to take that away, apply it and come back stronger for as long as we are able to continue.'

Ashley is looking forward to getting glammed up for the show and says the more sequins the better.

'Let's do this!' she laughs. 'Bring on the sparkles, honey.'

Former champ Pasha Kovalev is paired with Ashley Roberts for series 16, and he couldn't be happier. 'When I was told I had Ashley I got really excited,' he says. 'I think she will be one of those contenders in the competition who might surprise everyone with her ballroom skills.'

While she has danced before as a member of The Pussycat Dolls, Pasha warns that Ashley still has a lot to learn.

'When it comes to ballroom and Latin, it doesn't matter how much experience you have before, it will still feel like you are learning a brand-new skill, because the technique is completely different and the posture is different,' he says. 'Keeping that posture, especially in ballroom dances, is quite challenging.

'Ashley thinks that Latin will suit her better and she likes faster dances, but my goal is to bring that classy side out and prove to her that she can be a ballroom queen as well.'

Siberian-born Pasha started dancing at the age of eight. In 2001, he moved to the US to compete and, after turning professional. He joined *Strictly* in 2011 and has reached the Final three times, lifting the 2014 trophy with Caroline Flack.

Last year, Pasha was partnered with Chizzy Akudolu, but sadly they were the first couple to be eliminated.

'Chizzy and I did our absolute best and she performed so well. She gave her heart and soul to it, so I wouldn't do anything differently if we could go back.

Chizzy had rhythm, she had charisma, she had personality and I wish everyone could have seen more of her on *Strictly*.'

For Pasha, the launch show – when the professionals find out who they will be dancing with – is the 'most nerve-wracking part' of the series.

'Once you know who your partner is then everything settles in the right place because you know what route you are going to take, what kind of things you have to work on and hopefully how to bring the best dances out of them. After that, there is only excitement about the rehearsals and excitement for the series.

'I really look forward to seeing what kind of ballroom and Latin dancer I can mould out of Ashley and showing her what *Strictly* is all about.'

But Pasha admits there is plenty of competition this year.

'I look at everyone dancing in the group routines and I notice that there are so many potentially good dancers among the men and women this time around, so we have a very close competition ahead of us. It will be interesting to see how it all plays out.'

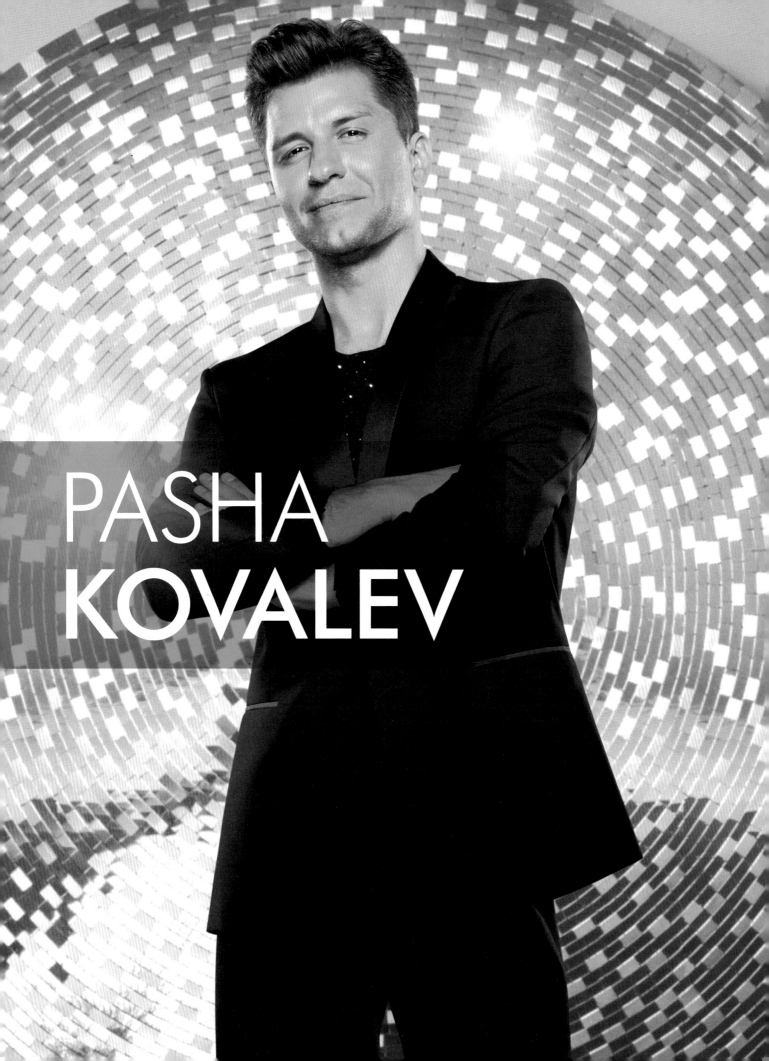

PASHA
KOVALEV

From her sofa in the *It Takes Two* studio, Zoë Ball casts an expert eye over *Strictly* proceedings every year. And she is delighted with the class of 2018.

'What a line-up,' she says. 'There are some very promising partnerships that made me squeal with delight. You can't not have your eye on Vick and Graziano – double delight. Susannah and Anton make for a fun pairing and Giovanni and Faye could be smashing. Also, Charles and Karen look like a dynamic duo, and I'm seeing good things for Danny John-Jules. There's going to be some brilliant routines coming up.'

As a former contestant as well as being the *It Takes Two* presenter, Zoë has a unique view on the dances and what goes on behind the scenes. And she knows exactly how the celebrity contestants feel ahead of their first few dances.

'Those first few lessons are equal parts excitement and fear. It just doesn't seem like you're ever going to master those steps, your feet and thighs are killing you, but then the wonder that is your teacher and partner will fill you with self-belief and confidence and you fall completely in love with dance.'

Zoë and dance partner Ian Waite made it to the Final in series three but lost out to Darren Gough and Lilia Kopylova. But she had such a ball that she still experiences a pang of envy as the new celebrities take to the floor.

'I'm absolutely jealous,' she admits. 'It's the best adventure ever and I think the music, staging, costumes and choreography gets better and better each year. But the standard is so high, I'm glad I did it years ago when I was more flexible. I'm not sure my body would cope now. I'm still gutted that Ian and I never got to do the Argentine Tango and Charleston, though.'

Zoë has some sound advice for the quaking contestants. 'Throw yourself into it, relish every moment, believe in your partner and try not to worry about the people at home watching.'

This will be Zoë's eighth year in the hotseat and she has some treasured memories from last year's *Strictly* and *It Takes Two*.

'Last year had some unforgettable routines,' she says. 'I particularly loved Debbie McGee's Paso Doble, Joe McFadden's Viennese Waltz, Alexandra Burke's Jive and Aston Merrygold's Cha-cha-cha troll dance. The Final was an epic battle – I wanted them all to win.

'My favourite moments on *It Takes Two* were dancing with Ian Waite. I adore him. And he makes me laugh so, so much. Also, last year Vincent Simone danced the Argentine Tango with me, and although there is a serious height difference, he made me feel like a queen.'

This year, Zoë is back on *It Takes Two*, giving avid fans a *Strictly* fix in between the weekend shows. She'll be joined by regulars Ian Waite, Neil Jones and Gethin Jones and promises the usual backstage news and fun.

'There will be more daft dance nonsense with all your favourites and the pro dancers teaching everyone at home some new moves,' she says.

'I'm looking forward to catching up with the pros and watching the new friendships grow. It's the best people-watching ever.

'It will also be interesting to meet the three new professionals. The new dancers have a lot to live up to . . . bring it on.'

ZOE BALL

GRAEME
SWANN

The world of cricket has already thrown up two *Strictly* champs, in Mark Ramprakash and Darren Gough. But England star Graeme Swann doesn't feel he has to live up to past glories.

'I don't feel any pressure at all,' he says. 'Mark Ramprakash is amazing, and Darren Gough is brilliant, but although the last two were fun (Phil Tufnell and Michael Vaughan) I'm not sure they were the greatest dancers. They're really good mates of mine, so I can say that. From my point of view my glass is half full. It's time we got the cricketers back to the top of the tree.'

Graeme was born in Northampton and began his career playing for the county team before moving to Nottinghamshire in 2005. As part of the England squad, he was instrumental in bringing home the Ashes in 2009. In the same year, he became the first English spin bowler to take 50 wickets in one calendar year. In 2010, in a Test against Bangladesh, he became the first English off-spinner in 60 years to take 10 wickets in a match and was named ECB Cricketer of the Year. He retired from cricket in 2013 and is now a BBC pundit.

Graeme, who is partnered with Oti Mabuse, has no dance experience, but learning ballroom is a long-held ambition.

'I've always harboured a secret desire to know how to dance,' he says. 'At weddings, grandparents always used to get up and waltz and that whole generation could dance, but that's gone. People don't learn to dance any more. I've always wanted to do that, so that was why I wanted to do *Strictly*.

'Last year my little boy asked to go to bed early one Friday so he could stay up to watch *Strictly* on Saturday, so I'm doing it for him and for my other two kids. I want to be superdad. They're over the moon, they're absolutely buzzing.'

They also think Dad can bring home the trophy. 'Absolutely, they think I'm going to win,' laughs Graeme. 'They're seven, five and two. They still think I can fly!'

The former bowler hopes that his sporting prowess will make that wish come true.

'When you train and compete for a living you get used to it; it drives you and it'll drive me on *Strictly* without a doubt. I want to be in it as far as I can possibly go and surprise myself.'

Graeme is keen to learn the Waltz and, if he nails it, wife Sarah might be in for a nice surprise.

'I've got this romantic notion of a moonlit square in Rome and music playing and just taking the wife by the hand and waltzing round. It'll never happen, obviously – we've got young kids. They'd be running around eating pizza. But that classic film moment would be gorgeous.'

Graeme has embraced the fake tan and sequins. 'I'm more than happy with it!', he says. 'Bring it on!'

South African dancer Oti Mabuse was bowled over when she was paired with cricketer Graeme Swann, because it came as a total surprise. 'I really didn't expect it,' she said. 'This year I was so relaxed, I said I would be really happy with any of them. I don't know anything about cricket so it was nice to just get to know him as him, rather than the celebrity persona.

'I think he will be a lot of fun. I'm excited about this whole journey that we are going to go on. He comes across as very energetic. It seems like he wants to dance and he's very positive, so that's exciting.'

Oti began dancing as a young child, following in the footsteps of her sister Motsi, who is now a judge on the German version of Strictly. After becoming South African Latin American Champion eight times, Oti moved to Germany to find new challenges. She has achieved many titles in her dancing career, including World European Latin semi-finalist and World Cup Championship semi-finalist.

Last year, Oti danced with Paralympian Jonnie Peacock and says he was an inspiration.

'Dancing with Jonnie was exciting to discover this whole new world,' she says. 'Jonnie introduced me to a new mentality, and showed me the lengths that people will go to in order to be great, and he's an absolute champion.

This season, Oti is welcoming another old friend, Johannes Radebe, into the professional dance group.

'Johannes and I grew up together and we used to compete against each other. We competed against rival provinces as well,' she reveals.

'I am so excited he is joining Strictly, he is like an undiscovered talent – one of many that we have in South Africa – and I know that people will open up their hearts to him.'

Oti – who danced with Olympic boxer Anthony Ogogo in her first Strictly series in 2015 – is looking forward to partnering a sportsman once again.

'Graeme is the third athlete,' she says. 'Apart from Danny Mac, I've only partnered athletes in the show, but it's different with every single one.'

OTI
MABUSE

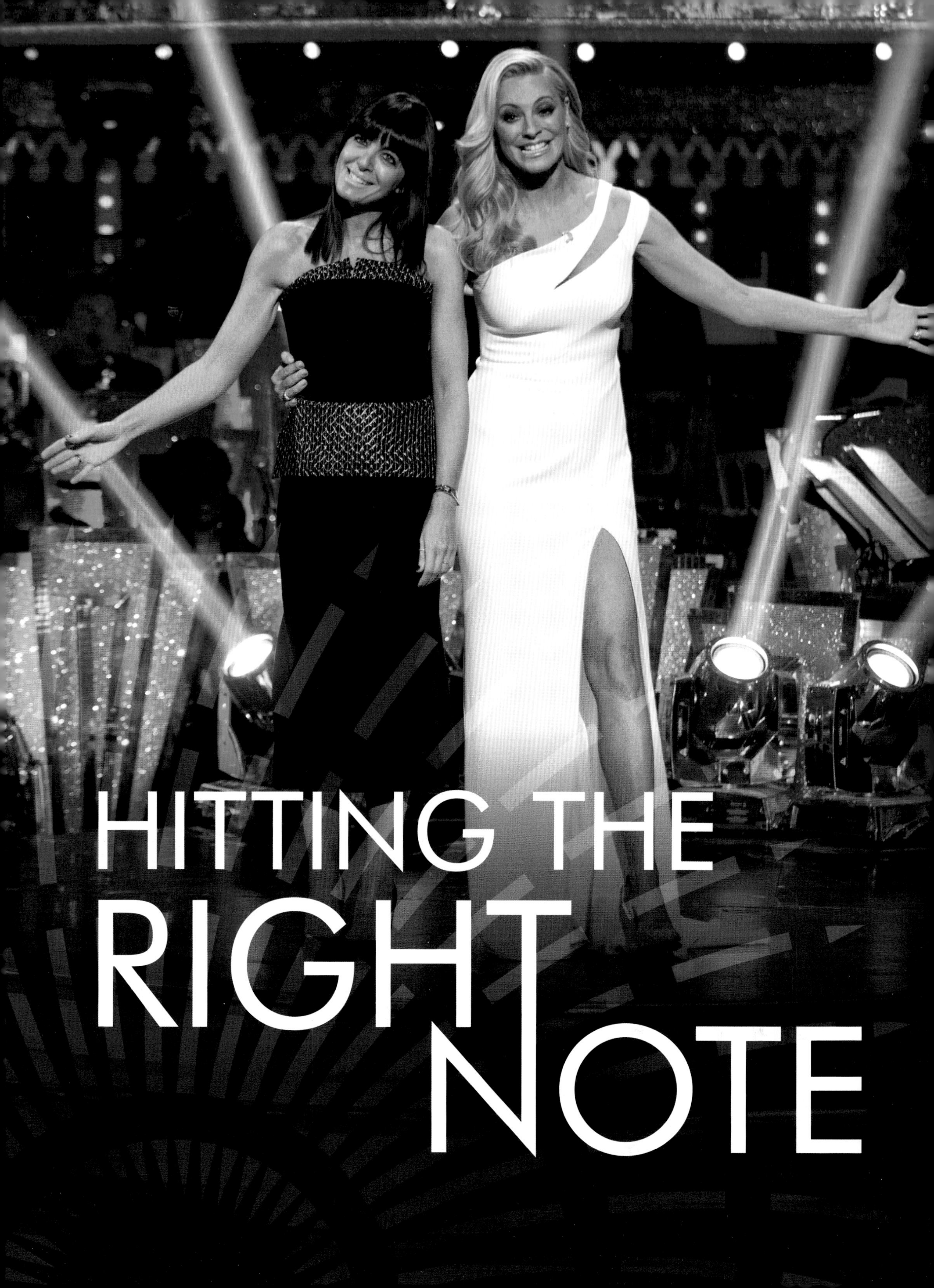

HITTING THE RIGHT NOTE

Da-da-da-da-da-da-da, da-da-da-da-da! As soon as the opening bars of the theme tune play on Saturday night, *Strictly* fans know it's time to settle in for a great show. It's as familiar to viewers as Bruno Tonioli falling off his chair.

For composers Dan McGrath and Josh Phillips, who came up with the iconic tune 14 years ago, it's still a thrill to hear.

'I go to the live show with my daughter and you can feel the excitement as soon as the music starts,' says Josh. 'People say it makes them feel good and every time it strikes up at the arena, you can see and hear the response. All around, you hear people going, "Da-da-da-da-da-da-da ..."'

Dan and Josh came up with the theme tune after being approached by BBC Producer Richard Hopkins in 2004.

'Richard told us they were working on a show that would be like *Come Dancing* but with celebrities,' recalls Dan. 'I used to watch *Come Dancing* back in 1972, and I couldn't see how it was going to work, but we knew Bruce Forsyth was presenting so it had the potential to be big.

'We had a blank canvas as far as musicality was concerned, but we knew it was prime-time TV, it's Saturday night, it's dancing, it's showbiz and it's for the whole family.

'Over the years Josh and I have learned the tricks and the instruments to include, and with a show like this it's all about pizzazz and sparkle. We wanted a call to action so that someone in the kitchen would hear it and instantly know that the show was about to start. That's why the intro comes in with the "bam-bam". We had that from the very early stages.'

'We tried various dance styles, but the

Cha-cha-cha beat seemed perfect,' Josh explains. 'Latin American is so addictive, it has a party vibe and it's very modern. Plus, you can use the drum for the rhythm, which works well. So we used the Latin rhythm as a springboard and we built it up from there.'

The duo created the track electronically in their studio, layering different sounds onto the Latin base. In total, they came up with eight versions before they hit the jackpot.

'At version five we had a solid version,' says Dan, 'but it wasn't bright enough. It was a bit boring, and we needed to up the attack. We added a muted trumpet, which has a very specific sound. But the top line wasn't there, and that's when we created the "da-da-da-da-da-da-da, da-da-da-da-da" that everybody knows.'

'It was quite simplistic, but that's what made it hummable and instantly recognisable,' adds Josh.

Apart from the muted trumpet, instruments that can be heard on the track include bass percussion, bass guitar, acoustic guitar, piano,

electric guitar, a string pad, a synthesiser and brass.

'Then there's somebody in the background going, "Oh!" and "Hey!"' laughs Josh. 'That was Dan, shouting from the back of the studio.'

But the secret ingredient is the audience itself.

'It got to the point where it was almost there but needed that extra little detail to push it over the top and make it more exciting,' says Dan. 'We wanted a sound effect that would make everybody jump up and take notice as soon as the music started, so we came up with an audience clapping and cheering, right at the start. It's not loud enough to be obtrusive, but it's just enough to sell it and add a celebratory touch.'

After the final track was signed off, Laurie Holloway and his orchestra, the original house band on the show, attempted to record the track, but, Dan reveals, 'It didn't sound like the demo, so we reverted back to what we had done in the studio.'

The recording Dan and Josh submitted 14

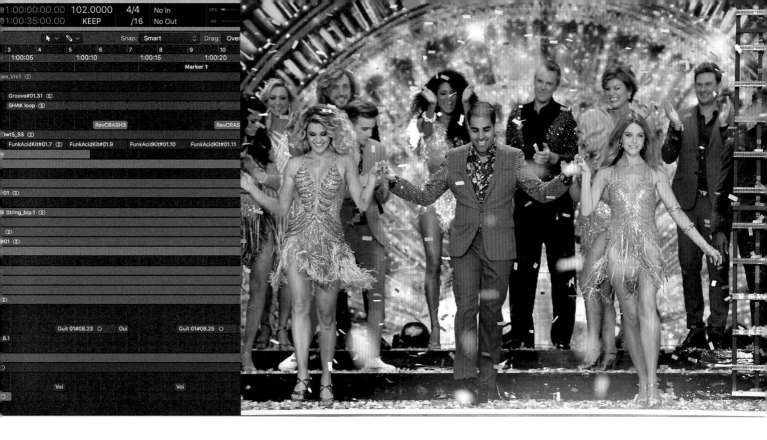

years ago is still heard by viewers today. It also opens *Dancing with the Stars* in countries around the world.

'We didn't know how long the show was going to last and to still be hearing the theme tune 14 years on is ridiculous but fantastic,' says Josh. 'It's a good, solid tune and it's so synonymous with the show. To have something like that, where it's so identifiable and it means such a lot to people, is wonderful.

'I play with a band and every time we do a live gig I slip a few bars of the *Strictly* tune in somewhere. It couldn't be further removed from the band's music, but it brings the house down.'

As well as being loved by millions of *Strictly* fans, the tune has netted the talented duo 10 awards from ASCAP (the American Society of Composers, Authors and Publishers) and won praise from one very distinguished quarter.

'Tony Hatch, who wrote the *Neighbours* theme tune and some of the most memorable TV theme tunes ever, did an interview a couple of years back and he was asked if there were any current TV themes that stood out for him,' recalls Dan. 'He said, "I would have to say *Strictly Come Dancing*. It's got what I would call a 'fatal opening'."

'To have Tony Hatch pick that as the current theme tune that stood out for him was amazing. You can't beat that.

'When I was 14, I was into synthesisers and I was going to be in a band, and then I wanted to be on *Top of the Pops,* but that was not to be. Ironically, Josh and I have written a piece that is universally recognised and there are people in the middle of nowhere, singing the tune we created 14 years ago and loving it. That's a really great feeling.

'When you listen to old TV themes, like *The Professionals* or *The Sweeney,* there is an emotional response and we have made a tune that, I hope, people will hear in 30 years' time and have the same response. Mind you, *Strictly* could still be on the telly then!'

FAYE TOZER

Faye Tozer may be used to 'Steps', but Latin and ballroom is a whole new area of dance for her.

'I'm quite excitable when I'm on stage, so I'm good at jumping around,' she admits. 'But there are so many details that go into ballroom dancing and Latin; it's not just throwing a few shapes. You have to grab onto someone and they have to lead you around. My biggest comment from the male partners in group rehearsal was that I'm not very good at being led.'

Faye was born in Northampton and first had the nation tapping its toes when Steps released their catchy debut '5, 6, 7, 8' in 1997. The group went on to sell 25 million records, including 15 million albums, before splitting in 2001. After years of reunion talk they finally got back together to tour in 2012. Last year they appeared on Strictly's Halloween Week – which left Faye yearning for a turn on the dance floor.

'Strictly is the most fabulous show on telly and one I've had my eye on for years, so the appearance last year just made me want it more,' she says. 'I'm over the moon that I'm finally getting to do it.

'I was on holiday in Portugal when I heard. I was just walking down the street with my husband, got the phone call and I literally balled my eyes out – I was in shock. I was so amazed and so happy. It was brilliant, absolutely wonderful.'

Faye was sworn to secrecy for the summer and had no idea that friend and fellow pop star Lee Ryan would also be on the show.

'We just spent the summer together,' says Faye. 'Blue were supporting Steps on our summer tour, but we didn't tell each other that we were doing this, so it was a surprise when we both found out. It's lovely that he is on the show at the same time.'

Faye, who will dance with Giovanni Pernice, says there's no rivalry between herself and her fellow competitors.

'There's no competition yet,' she says. 'During group dance rehearsals there was just massive camaraderie because we all had the fear. Just getting the group dance learned has brought us together.

'It's interesting to see who the movers are, and how passionate people are. Stacey makes me laugh and that girl can move. And Charles has got amazing hips. You're going to love those hips.'

Faye is equally excited about the ballroom and the Latin and is particularly keen to learn the Tango. But she admits to a touch of nerves.

'My biggest fear is blanking in the middle of a routine and forgetting where I am,' she says. 'I won't have the audience doing the moves back to me this time. It's going to be just me on my own.'

After making it to the Final with Debbie McGee last year, Giovanni Pernice will be stepping out with Steps star Faye Tozer this season. The ever-modest, cheeky Italian says he was thrilled with the pairing – and the feeling was mutual. 'I am really pleased to be partnered with Faye. When she got paired with me she was really happy,' he laughs. 'Why would you not be? She's only human!'

Although Faye's Steps routines came with choreographed moves, Giovanni doesn't believe that will help her when it comes to ballroom and Latin.

Ballroom and Latin is hard for her, because she now has a technique to learn and it's completely different. As with every year with my celebrity, they don't have an idea what it is all about, so we need to be really patient and try to teach them how to dance, which is our job.

'But I think Faye is going to be incredible in everything. After all, she's got the best teacher!'

Giovanni was born in Sicily and started dance lessons at a young age. At 14, he moved to Bologna to attend dance school. His greatest achievement is the day he won the Italian Championships in 2012. Giovanni joined *Strictly* in 2015, reaching the Final with actress Georgia May Foote. He repeated the feat last year with Debbie, making it two Final appearances in three seasons.

'I was really pleased to be in the Final with Debbie. I really found a friend for life. Of course, dancing-wise she was phenomenal, but she was also a really good friend and we had an amazing time.'

While he's hoping for a hat-trick – and his first win – Giovanni says the competition is stiff this season.

'There are so many good dancers. The standard is higher this year, 100 per cent. Everybody can dance and lots are really good dancers, so it will be difficult. But that's better for me. I'm really competitive so I like it. I wouldn't want it to be easy.'

GIOVANNI
PERNICE

GUESS THE DRESS

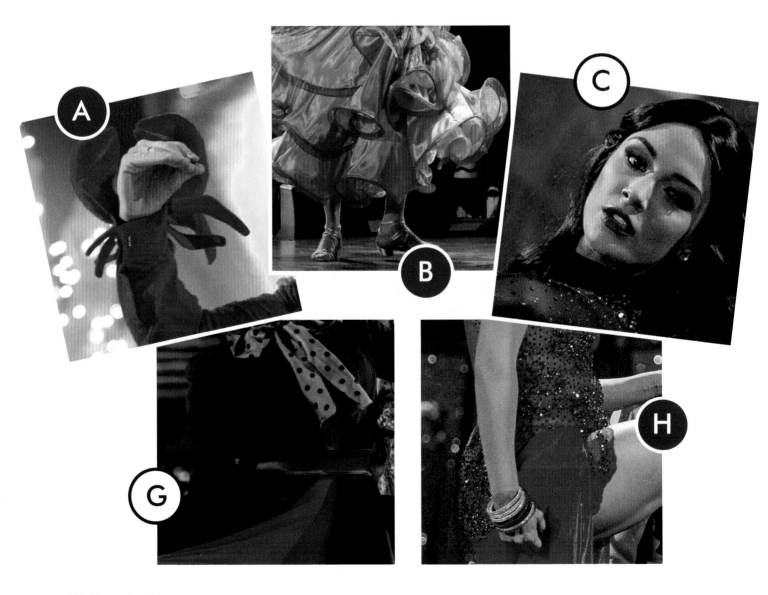

Since *Strictly Come Dancing* began, the wardrobe department has created over 2,000 amazing costumes for the celebrities alone. While each is as elegant and stylish as the next, there are some that will be never be forgotten.

The shots below are close-ups of some of the show's most iconic outfits. Can you name the celebrities who wore them?

GUESS THE DRESS

A. Scott Mills, crab (Samba, 2015)

B. Ann Widdecombe's yellow-and-red Flamenco dress (Paso Doble, 2010)

C. Frankie Bridge, green-faced *Wicked* dance (Tango, 2014)

G. Alexandra Burke as Mary Poppins (Charleston, 2017)

H. Debbie McGee's red dress (Paso Doble, 2017)

I. Ore Oduba's striped suit (Charleston, Halloween Special 2017)

D. Ed Balls as *The Mask* (Samba, 2016)

E. Danny Mac's red suit 'Puttin' on the Ritz' (Charleston, 2016)

F. Caroline Flack's 'Istanbul' (Charleston, 2014 Final)

J. Gemma Atkinson's 'Bare Necessities' (Charleston, 2017)

K. Anita Rani as Maleficent (Waltz, 2015)

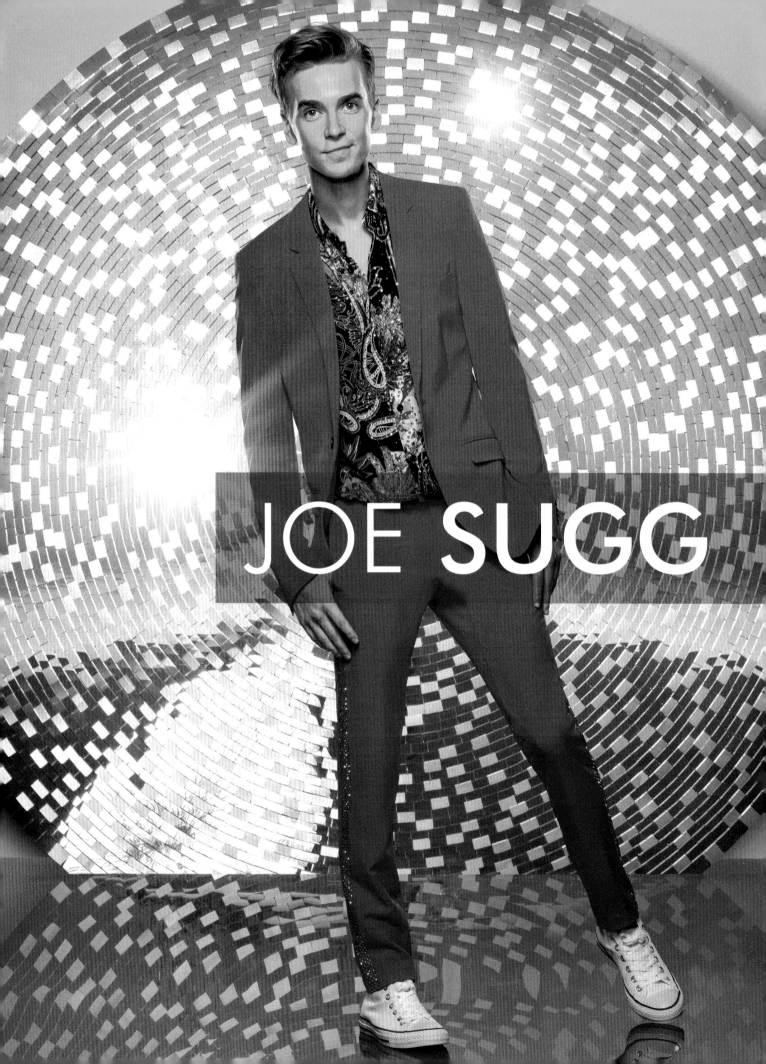

JOE SUGG

Joe Sugg was just 12 when *Strictly Come Dancing* first hit UK screens and he has grown up watching the show. So he didn't have to think twice about signing up.

'I had this giant pros list and a very small cons list,' he says. 'It's always been a big thing within our family, so it's very exciting. My grandparents love it and it was a nice surprise for them to see their grandson giving it a go. It'll be a massive confidence booster as well and my mates will love it.

'Also, it's learning a new skill. I haven't really thought about dancing in that way before, but now I think it'll be nice to learn how to dance. All my friends back home are getting married, so it'd be nice to go along and be able to dance. Obviously after the first dance – I don't want to steal the show!'

Joe, from Lacock, Wiltshire, is a popular vlogger who set up his YouTube channel in 2011. His videos, containing a mixture of comedy, impressions and pranks, have earned him a following of over 13 million. In 2015, he made a TV show with Caspar Lee, entitled *Joe & Caspar Hit the Road*, and he also provided the voice of a seagull in *The SpongeBob Movie*.

His older sister is Zoe Sugg, better known as the beauty blogger and author Zoella, and Joe jokes that he is best known for being 'Zoella's brother'.

'I did a charity football game recently and we had to pick a name for the back of our shirts. I chose "Zoella's Brother". I don't like to take myself too seriously. I just take things as they come.

'Zoe's really excited about *Strictly*, though. Hopefully she'll come down and watch.'

Although he says he's not a natural dancer, Joe – who is dancing with Dianne Buswell – isn't worried about the judges.

'I keep forgetting that we're going to get judged by the four judges,' he says. 'I know that I'm definitely not the most capable dancer, so it can only get better.

'I think if the judges do give me feedback, I'll really take it on board and make sure it never happens again.'

After being paired with YouTube star Joe Sugg, Dianne Buswell is helping him make the transition from filming in the comfort of his own home to performing in front of a live audience.

'On the launch show I felt Joe's nerves and I felt that he was out of his comfort zone,' she reveals. 'But as soon as we started rehearsing he gained confidence, and every day we rehearse he comes out of his shell a bit more, so I don't have any worries about that any more. I think he'll give it his full personality and people are going to love him.'

Dianne says she and Joe are 'having a ball' in training and she is happy with her pupil's progress so far.

'It's very exciting. We get on so well,' she says. 'Joe is probably the person I danced with the least in the group dance, so we didn't really get to know each other before we were paired, but I already feel like I've known him forever. We have a very similar sense of humour, so we are laughing so much together and having a good time.

'I'm very impressed with him. He has a beautiful long neck, which might sound odd but for ballroom dancing the top line is crucial and I think his will be really good. Also, he picks up choreography fast and he doesn't forget. He will get the steps, but it's doing everything all together that might be the hardest thing. It's more about polishing the performance, because I really do feel like there's a little dancer within.'

Dianne was born in Bunbury, Australia, and started dancing at four. Partnered by brother Andrew, she won the Australian Open Championships and was a four-time Open finalist.

Last year, Dianne made a memorable *Strictly* debut dancing with the Reverend Richard Coles, although they were the second couple to leave.

'My favourite moment of last year was the first dance with Rev, the Cha-cha-cha to "There Must Be an Angel", when he came down on a cloud. It was such a joyous moment. It was my first dance, his first dance and it was very special. I loved that.

'Last year was a massive learning curve. This year I'm going into it knowing what to expect. I'm hoping to push Joe all the way to the Final and I feel like he really wants to get there as well. It's going to be exciting.'

DIANNE
BUSWELL

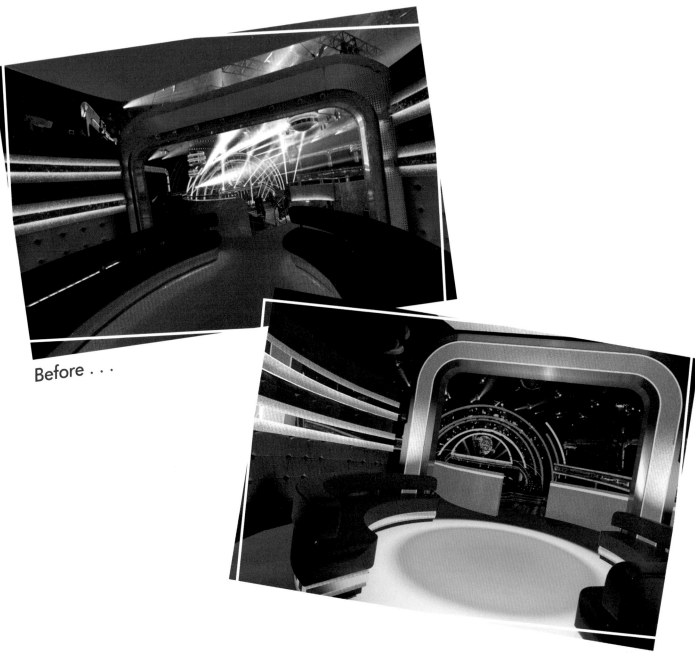

Before · · ·

· · · After

SETTING THE SCENE

Since moving to Elstree Studios in 2013, the *Strictly* set has stayed largely the same, with a few small tweaks that only the most eagle-eyed of viewers would spot. This year, however, a new colour scheme has been introduced, and while the differences are subtle in the main studio, viewers may have noticed a more radical makeover in one important area – the Clauditorium.

The area where Claudia Winkleman greets the couples at the end of their routines has been updated with a new look. Gone are the rich purple-and-silver walls and the red-lit floor, and in comes a clean blue-and-gold redesign.

It's all part of a fresher look which follows on from the red-carpet event at the start of the series when the celebrities are introduced, as set designer Patrick Doherty explains.

'Overall, the whole vibe of the series is a bit more contemporary,' he says. 'So, with the red-carpet event at New Broadcasting House we installed columns of screen and an LED structure at the end, which opened to reveal the stars.

'In the past we have had the celebrities arriving in a train, and we've launched a rocket, and that part of the show gets bigger every year. Last year we did something quite romantic, with palm trees and a nod to the suave and sophisticated, to Miami in the 1930s. This year it was much more contemporary chic.'

The rest of the studio, Patrick reveals, remains structurally the same and the biggest change comes from the clever use of the LED screens that provide the backdrop to all the celebrity and professional dances.

'The main change is the colour palette,' he says. 'Of course, that will depend on the routines, but it's a tweaked version of last year, with more aqua shades and less red and gold. The aquas, greens and blues will transfer onto the look of the set so that the overall dynamic will be nearer to the current logo.'

The redesign in Claudia's area is a reflection of this new colour scheme. The purple-and-silver walls have been replaced with a vibrant blue-and-gold design, the dark sofas re-upholstered in purple velvet and the red floor lighting has been switched to a turquoise glow.

'The new colour scheme is designed to lift the area and make it feel a bit fresher, and closer to the palette of the rest of the show.

'When you think of *Strictly* you tend to think of reds and golds and, although we still have a red drape providing the main background of the studio, the new graphics are more vibrant for a more modern look.'

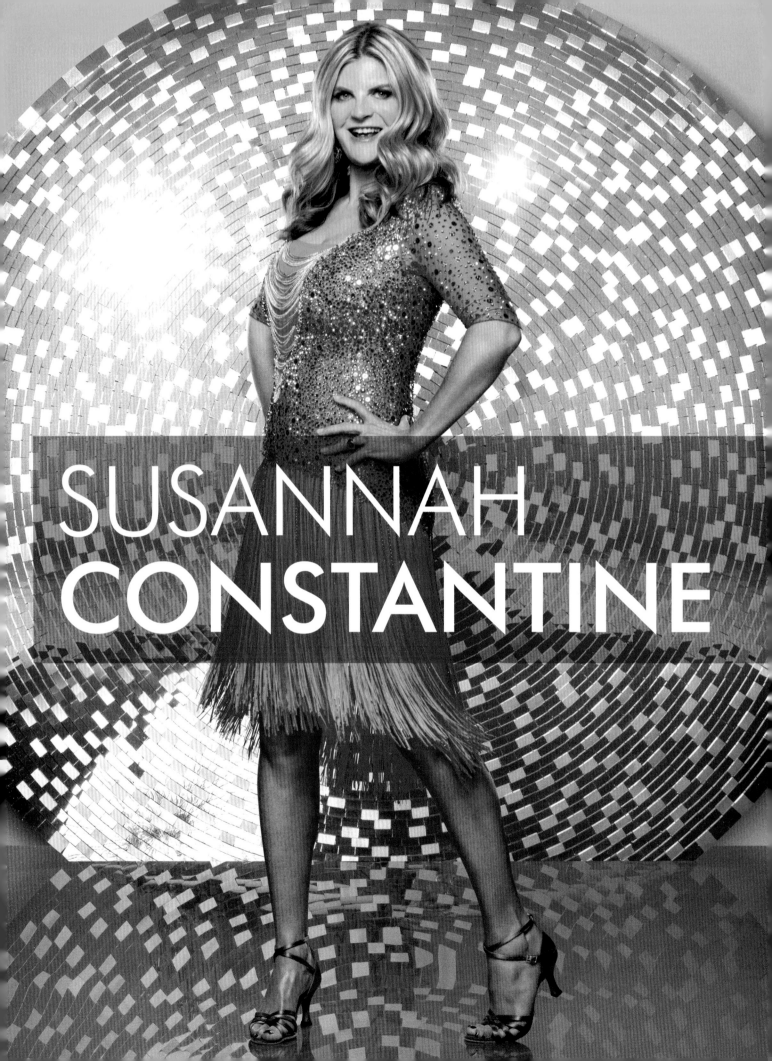

SUSANNAH
CONSTANTINE

As a fashionista, Susannah Constantine is in her element when it comes to sequins, stones and *Strictly* sparkle.

'For me, this is genuinely a dream come true. I have always watched *Strictly* and adored the clothing, because it's like being in a couture studio. I have worked with the best of the best and these people are right up there.

'I really believe that designers should take note of how they dress women. They appreciate women's bodies and understand women's bodies, and the way the designers flatter your shape is amazing. I am loving that, and I am in Wardrobe as much as I possibly can be – it's my happiest place.'

Susannah worked as a nursery nurse and a Harrods shopping assistant before falling into fashion, working for such household names as Giorgio Armani and John Galliano. She moved into journalism and broadcasting, teaming up with Trinny Woodall to write a *Daily Telegraph* column for seven years before moving to the BBC to launch the hit TV show *What Not to Wear*.

Now Susannah, who is partnered by Anton Du Beke, is keen to add another string to her bow by honing her ballroom and Latin skills.

'I just want to be able to dance one dance without people laughing at me,' she says. 'I have a heartfelt, genuine desire to dance and where better to learn than here?'

Although she has never danced before, Susannah says she is not letting nerves get the better of her when she faces the live shows.

'It's about compartmentalising everything and living in the actual moment and not winding the movie forward,' she says. 'If I think about that first live dance too much, I'd just run. You just have to stay in the moment.'

'I really want to impress the female judges because I have so much respect for them. It's like being a little girl all over again. You want to do well in their eyes and I want to please them, so I really hope I get a good comment from Darcey and Shirley.'

Susannah is expecting a lot of support from her children Joe, Esme and Cece as well as best friend and partner in fashion Trinny.

'Trinny was the first person I told that I was going to be on the show and she said to me, "Oh my gosh, you'll be brilliant." But I don't think she meant the dancing …'

Since joining in the first series, Anton Du Beke has delivered many of the golden moments in *Strictly* history – from Ann Widdecombe's *Titanic* Rumba and flying Tango to Nancy Dell'Olio's terrifying Halloween routine. But he's hoping his partnership with Susannah Constantine will be memorable because it gets him into the Final, for the second time since series one.

'I think there is a long run for us, because she is absolutely brilliant,' he says. 'She has great form, lovely style, great enthusiasm and great timing. She also has a wonderful personality. She's one to watch.

'What I love the most is that she is really, really determined. All I want is someone who is enthusiastic and loves the show. Susannah is doing it because she is a massive fan. She wants to stay in it as long as possible and will show people that.'

Anton was born in Sevenoaks, Kent, to a Spanish mother and Hungarian father. Boxing and football were his favourite sports until he came to dancing at the relatively late age of 14. He trained in contemporary, jazz, ballet and modern theatre dance until, inspired by his idol Fred Astaire, he decided to specialise in ballroom.

In 1998 and 1999, Anton and dance partner Erin Boag won the New Zealand Championship. The pair joined *Strictly* for the first series in 2004. Erin left in 2010 and Anton is now the only professional dancer to compete in every series of *Strictly*.

Anton's previous partners include Ann Widdecombe, Jerry Hall, Nancy Dell'Olio, Judy Murray and Lesley Joseph. In 2015, Anton made it to the Grand Final for the first time in 13 series, with Radio 3 presenter Katie Derham. Last year, Anton danced with Ruth Langsford, and the couple were eliminated after a week-eight Foxtrot.

'Ruth is a fan, which brings enthusiasm, and she has the most wonderful sense of humour,' says Anton. 'She's just the loveliest person you would expect to meet and I loved spending time with her. The time we spent in the studio together rehearsing and laughing was wonderful. She is the most joyous person I've ever met. I enjoyed every second of it.'

ANTON
DU BEKE

STRICTLY CROSSWORD

Down

1. Mollie and AJ danced a tango to this Robert Palmer classic, '— to Love' (8)
2. Ms Rogers, one half of the greatest Hollywood dance act of all time (6)
3. 'Reach Out, — — There': Track Jay McGuiness danced a Cha-cha-cha to (3, 2)
4. First name of the former Spice Girl who competed in series four (4)
5. The symbols of written music that make up a musical score (5)
6. See 16 down
8. '— Sir, That's My Baby'. Classic track Tameka Empson and Gorka Márquez danced a Charleston to (3)
12. —down, informal American dance event (3)
14. — Waltz, classic ballroom dance (8)
16 and 6 down. Name of 2016 winner (3, 5)
17. The only judge to have appeared on *Strictly* who hasn't been a judge on the *Strictly* judging panel (6)
18. Mrs Jones, professional dancer who lifted the Glitterball in 2017 (5)
19. The first name of the Liberal Democrat politician who appeared on the 2010 Christmas Special (5)
20 down and 24 across. Singer who danced with Janette Manrara in series 13 (5, 5)
21. 'Beyond the —', Bobby Darin track that accompanied Susan Calman's American Smooth (3)
22. — dance, the UK version of 12 down (4)

Across

1. Latin American dance of the Gaucho (9, 5)
7. Mr Osmond, guest judge in 2014 (5)
9. '— the Flintstones': Track chosen for 17 down's Charleston (4)
10. *Waterloo Road* star Healey, who made the Final in series nine (7)
11 and 13 across. Professional partner of 10 across (5, 7)
15. Singer Jason, who was a finalist in series nine (7)
18. Mr Clifton (5)
20. The Paso Doble and Tango have plenty of this emotion (7)
23. Series 14 contestant Ms Munchetty (4)
24. See 20 down
25. Singer who made it to the 2017 Final (9, 5)

QUIZ

After 15 series of *Strictly*, you've all become proper ballroom boffins, and you certainly know your Fleckerl from your New Yorker. Now it's time to put your knowledge to the test and step up to the challenge of the *Strictly* quiz!

1. Which 'smokin'' movie character did Ed Balls portray in series 14's Movie Week?

2. Whose Jive did Craig Revel Horwood compare to 'a stork who'd been struck by lightning'?

3. Which professional partnered runner-up Danny Mac in series 14?

4. Which is the fastest of the ballroom dances?

5. Name the celebrity who danced a Charleston to 'Fat Sam's Grand Slam' in 2009.

6. Mollie King was the second member of The Saturdays to grace the *Strictly* dance floor. Which of her bandmates beat her to it?

7. Which two celebrities have scored the highest number of perfect scores in the history of *Strictly*?

8. Which celebrity was the first to get a perfect score in 2017?

9. Who leads the *Strictly* orchestra?

10. Which former *EastEnder* took his series-12 Salsa with Janette Manrara to the 'Max', scoring 35 in week two?

11. Which professional dancer has had the most appearances in the Final?

12. Which puppy-obsessed character did Shirley Ballas become on Halloween in 2017?

13. New dancer Graziano Di Prima hails from the same Italian island as Giovanni Pernice. But what is it called?

14. In which dance would you find a fleckerl?

15. Which singer walked through a ring of fire in her 2012 showdance?

Answers

1. The Mask 2. Jeremy Vine 3. Oti Mabuse 4. The Quickstep 5. Chris Hollins 6. Frankie Bridge 7. Caroline Flack and Danny Mac 8. Chizzy Akudolu 9. Dave Arch 10. Jake Wood 11. Kevin Clifton 12. Cruella de Vil 13. Sicily 14. Viennese Waltz 15. Kimberley Walsh

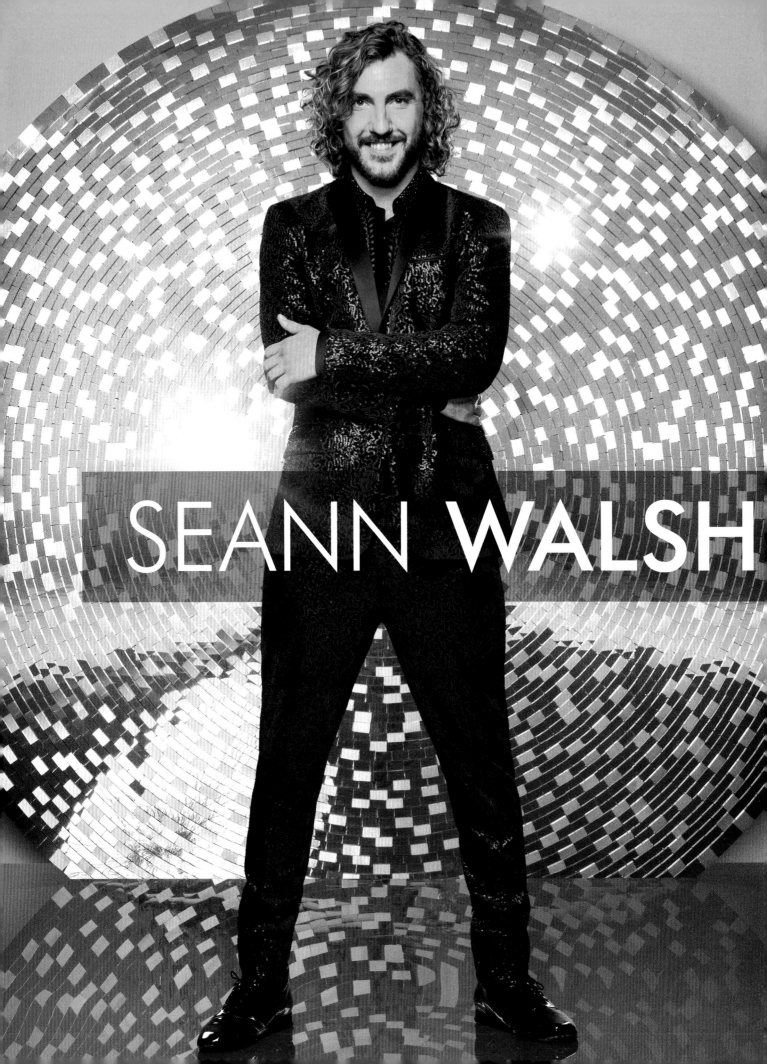

SEANN WALSH

Comedian Seann Walsh has been paired with current *Strictly* champ Katya Jones, but he reckons she's got her work cut out.

'I'm not just saying this but, when it comes to my dancing ability, we're starting at zero here. It's bad. I'm hoping that we start at zero and we go on a journey, but what I'm fearful of is that we start at zero and we end on zero.'

Self-deprecating as that might be, it seems his family and friends agree.

'I told my mum and the first thing she said was, "But, Seann, you can't dance,"' he reveals. 'And I've told my closest friends and all they've done is laugh very loudly and continuously for five minutes. Each and every one of them has had the same reaction.'

Seann, who grew up in Brighton, took to stand-up after graduating from Jill Edwards Comedy Workshops, performing his first gig in 2006. He got his big break when he supported Stephen K. Amos on his 2008 and 2009 tours, and in 2012 he toured with his own show, *Seann to Be Wild*, which he also performed at the Edinburgh Fringe Festival. He has since appeared in numerous TV and radio shows, including Jack Dee's sitcom *Bad Move*.

Despite his self-confessed lack of ability, Seann has a distant memory of a childhood dance class.

'For a small period of my life, when I was about seven, I did tap dancing at theatre school,' he recalls. 'They were teaching us to jump around like a frog and I remember thinking, "This is not what I want. I want to be Kevin Costner," so I dropped out.'

He's keen to learn from his dance partner Katya, saying 'I want to do *Strictly* because I want to learn how to dance,' and given his comedy background, Seann thinks the Charleston will be his best dance. 'You can do a load of silent comedy in a Charleston – a bit of slapstick.'

Current *Strictly* champ Katya Jones lifted the glitterball trophy last year with actor Joe McFadden. She made an instant impact in her 2016 *Strictly* debut, dancing with former minister Ed Balls, getting him to week ten with such memorable routines as the 'Gangnam Style' Salsa. This year she's up for more fun with comedian Seann Walsh.

'I have had two very different years, with Ed Balls and Joe, who are totally different characters, so this year I was ready for anything,' she says. 'With Seann I'm just having so much fun. He's a natural entertainer, so you might see us being a little bit silly and bringing lots of characters, but he is working so hard. He practises every single spare second.

'He says he is used to coming out and talking nonsense to people, but this is something he is going to take seriously. He wants to learn to dance properly. That's what all my partners have had so far and that's why we've done so well.'

Katya says she has been 'pleasantly surprised' by Seann in early rehearsals.

'So far his ballroom seems to be good,' she says. 'He's getting the frame and he really understands it. Maybe Latin will be a bit harder, because with the hips, the movement and the feet, there are a lot of things to think about. 'With Ed, I never compromised on steps or on technique, or let him stand still while I danced around, and that was the key. So this year, we will embrace the experience and not just try to be funny. I'm going to throw everything at Seann. No mercy!'

'Last year, when I won with Joe, hearing our names was crazy. It felt really rewarding. All those hours and the incredible amount of energy we had put in were all worth it in that moment.'

Katya was born in St Petersburg and started dancing at the age of six, training in gymnastics as well as ballroom and Latin American. In 2008, Katya started dancing with Neil Jones after meeting him in Blackpool, and they married in 2013. Together they won the World Amateur Latin Championships three times before turning professional and, in 2015, they became the World Professional Latin Showdance Champions. They are also the four-times undefeated British National Professional Champions.

KATYA
JONES

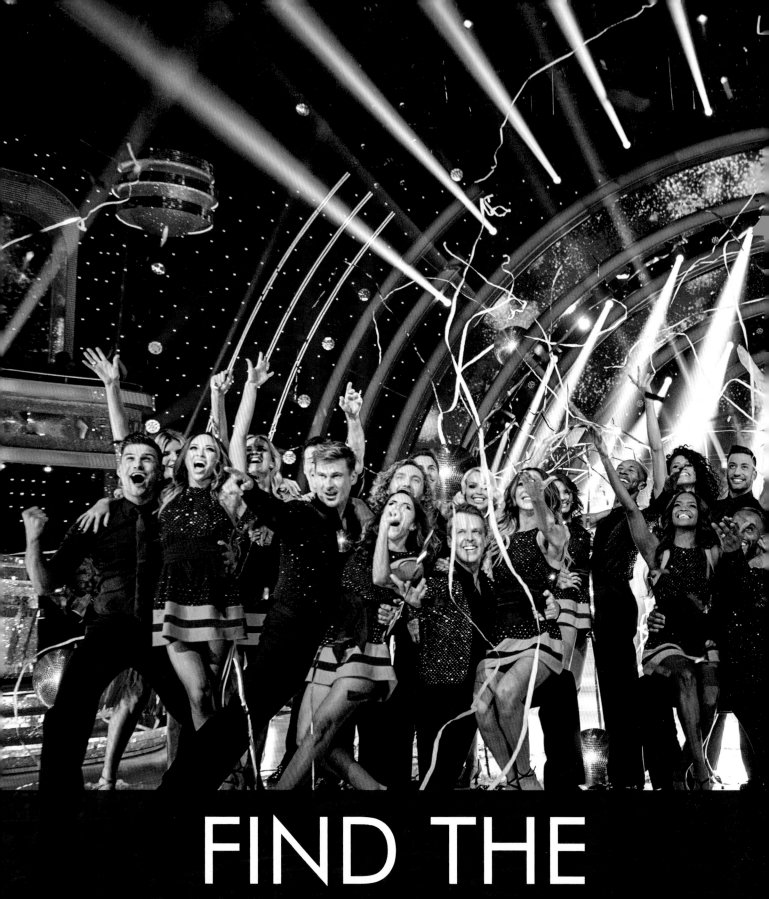

FIND THE
GLITTERBALL

The *Strictly* glitterball is always centre stage on the show, hanging above the dance floor for all to see. But the production crew have hidden 10 more mirrorballs around the set, until they are needed for a routine. Can you spot them? The sparkle ought to be enough to give them away. Turn to page 128 to find the answers . . .

Johannes Radebe may be new to Elstree, but he's no stranger to a *Strictly* dance floor, having reached the Final on the South African show.

'I did two seasons and I took both my partners to the Final,' he reveals. 'It was a huge thing for me and a very proud moment.'

Johannes grew up in a small town in South Africa and, at the age of seven, took up dancing.

'There were auditions for a new dance school and I told my mum I wanted to go and check it out, see what they were doing,' he says. 'I remember watching an elderly couple, fully dressed in the attire, and for me the sparkle, the elegance of the hold, the performance was something beautiful. From that day it was something I wanted to do.'

At nine, he started competing around the country – and winning. 'Every time I came home with a trophy and showed it to my mum, it brought her so much joy,' he recalls. 'I thought, "To make Mum proud, I'll keep doing it." I've never looked back.'

Johannes went on to become a two-time Professional South African Latin Champion and three-time Amateur South African Latin Champion. Joining the cast of *Strictly* was always an ambition.

'For me the goal was just to be part of this wonderful family,' he says. 'Now I'm here, every day I pinch myself because I still can't believe it. *Strictly* has given me a new purpose and I wake up every morning excited for what we are going to do today. It's awesome.

'The launch show was electrifying. It was incredible to see how people are invested in this show – the fans are amazing. The production value was unbelievable and I finally got to meet the judges I had only ever seen on TV. I was like a small boy – that excitement was beyond me.'

While he says all the professionals have helped him settle in, there was one familiar face he was especially keen to see.

'I used to compete against Oti back in the day. I have a vivid memory of a competition when we were very young. She had a leopard-print catsuit and big hair and it was such a statement look, coupled with fabulous dancing, because she was dynamic from a very young age.

'I've always wanted to dance with her, and now we are in the same group and I get to dance with her. It's exciting.

'Everybody has been so nice. It's lovely to work with them and learn from them. Anton told us we should enjoy the series and savour the moment, because there's nothing like it.'

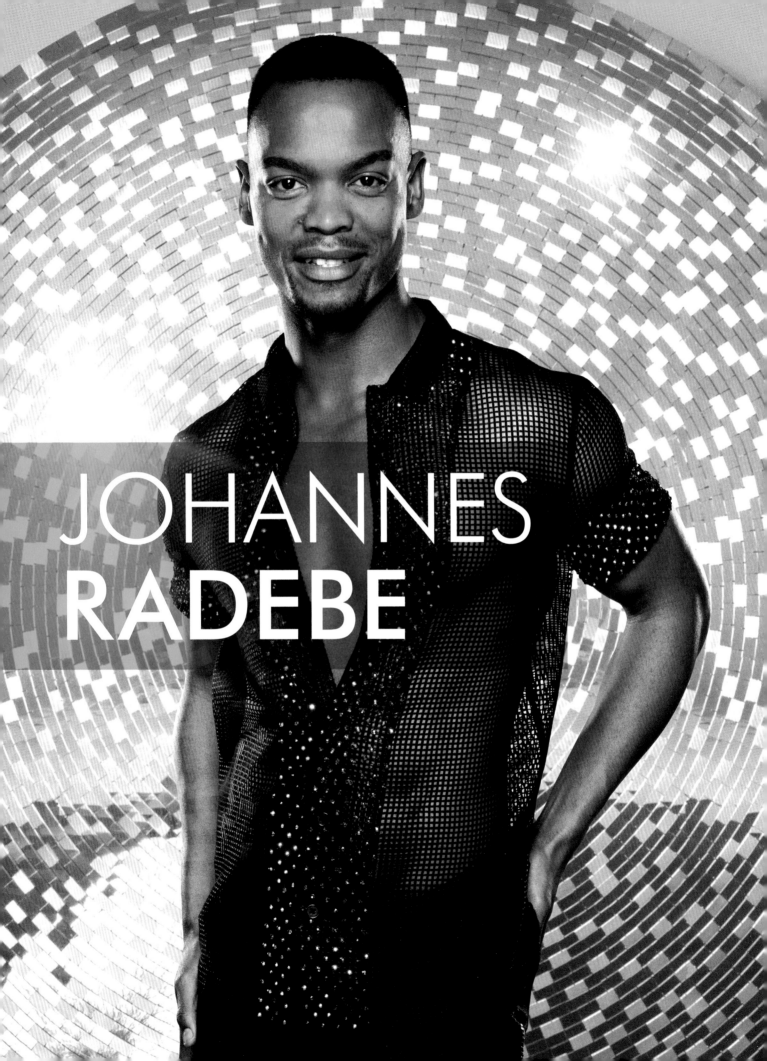

JOHANNES
RADEBE

Dancer and choreographer Neil Jones believes *Strictly* is gearing up for its best season ever, judging by the new-look launch show.

'I loved the launch show,' he says. 'I loved the fresh new style of it. It's still in keeping with what we normally do, but it also feels a little bit more modern. The group dances were all so good, I loved them all, but I especially liked the routine to "Havana" by Camila Cabello, because it is just a great song and the choreography was amazing.'

Neil was born in a British Army Camp in Munster, Germany, and started dancing at a local ballet school at the age of three. He trained in ballroom, Latin, tap, modern and ballet. Neil met wife Katya Jones in Blackpool in 2008 and they formed a dance partnership, becoming the undefeated four-time British National Champions and the three-time winners of the World Amateur Latin Championships. In 2015, Neil and Katya were crowned World Professional Latin Showdance Champions.

Although he is not dancing with a celebrity this year, Neil will have plenty to do. As well as taking part in all the group dances, he will be making his usual regular appearances on *It Takes Two* and choreographing the Children in Need special. He also danced with Judy Murray for a brilliant Charleston to 'Let's Misbehave' in last year's Christmas special.

'She was so good, so hard-working and willing to learn, so it was great. It wasn't so difficult to teach her the steps. Because she is a sporty person I knew I could push her more. She's used to repetition, so we could do it over and over again. She was improving every day, so I knew we were in a good place.'

Although they didn't win the trophy, tennis fan Neil got a little gift from his Christmas partner.

'I met Jamie Murray and I got to see Andy Murray play, so that was fantastic,' he said. 'That was the highlight of my year.'

For Children in Need, Neil was partnered with presenter Konnie Huq in a *Blue Peter* special, which was won by Mark Curry.

'Konnie was working so hard, we worked on it and we made sure the routine brought out the best in her.'

Another highlight of Neil's year was watching Katya bag the glitterball trophy in the Grand Final, with Joe McFadden.

'It was fantastic,' he says. 'Katya worked hard all year and she wasn't expecting it. She wasn't even thinking about it. She just wanted to make it as entertaining as possible and she nailed it.'

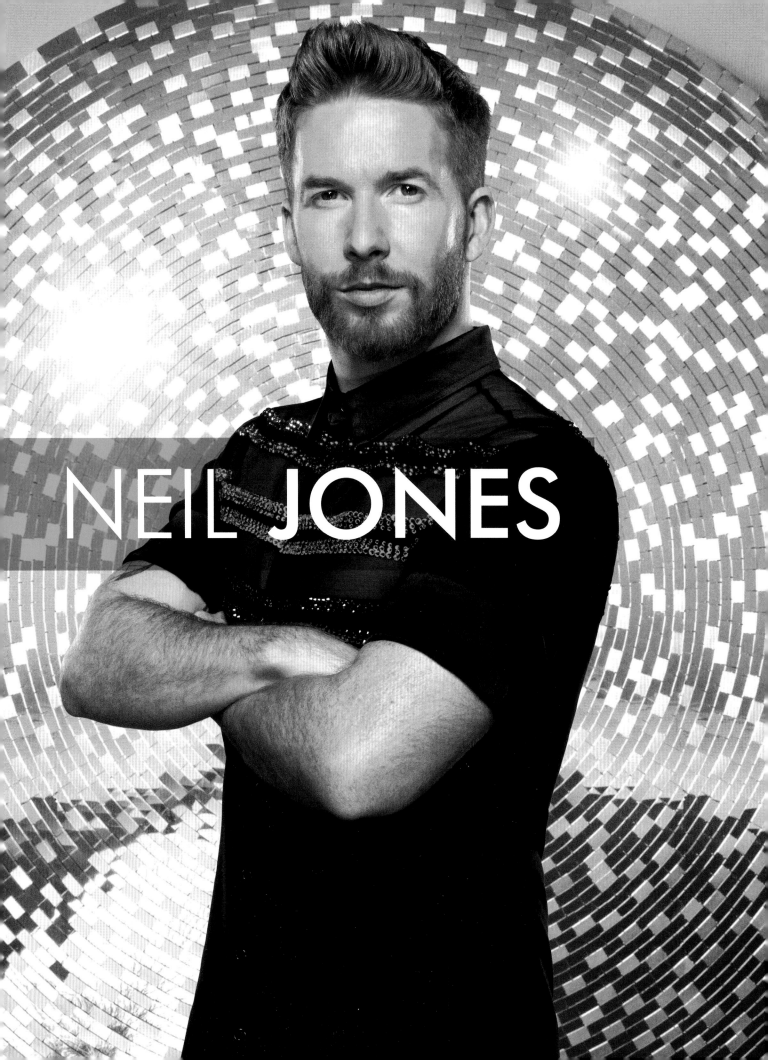

NEIL JONES

Although she is new to the professional dance troop, Luba Mushtuk is a familiar face on the *Strictly* set. For the last two years she has been assistant choreographer, working with head choreographer Jason Gilkison. Even so, she couldn't be more excited to be moving centre stage.

'I feel like when you are in love and you have all those butterflies in your stomach and you're extremely happy, but there's that tiny bit of nervousness,' she laughs. 'After two seasons of being behind the scenes, I know everybody really well, but this feels extremely different to my previous role. I'm feeling very excited.'

Luba was born in St Petersburg, Russia, and started competing in Latin and ballroom at the age of four. At just 12, she left home and travelled to Italy to study with 10-Dance World Champion Caterina Arzenton.

'I went back and forth for years because I had to finish my schooling,' she says. 'I remember travelling with a huge suitcase full of books. When I did my annual exams I would go back to Russia and have a few hours with the teacher to go through anything I didn't understand before the exam, but the rest of the time I travelled with my books and studied by myself. Luckily I have a very good memory, so I finished school well.'

The training paid off and Luba became four-time winner of the Italian Dance Championship and Italian Open Latin Show Dance Champion. She was ranked second in the European 10-Dance Championships and was a finalist in the Latin European Championship.

Competing took Luba all over the world. She lived in Hong Kong for some years while studying with another teacher and has also studied in the UK.

'The other day I found a picture of me in London when I was 13,' she says. 'I came to have lessons because many great teachers are here. England was always part of my travelling, so I feel quite at home in the UK.'

After a few years of competing, Luba moved into theatre. She has also danced in the *Strictly Come Dancing Live* tour.

Although she is not paired with a celebrity this year, Luba is thrilled to be dancing alongside the other professionals in the live shows.

'I am looking forward to sharing this experience with the 17 other incredible professional dancers who inspire me every day when I train with them. To just be able to do what I love on the best show on television is priceless.'

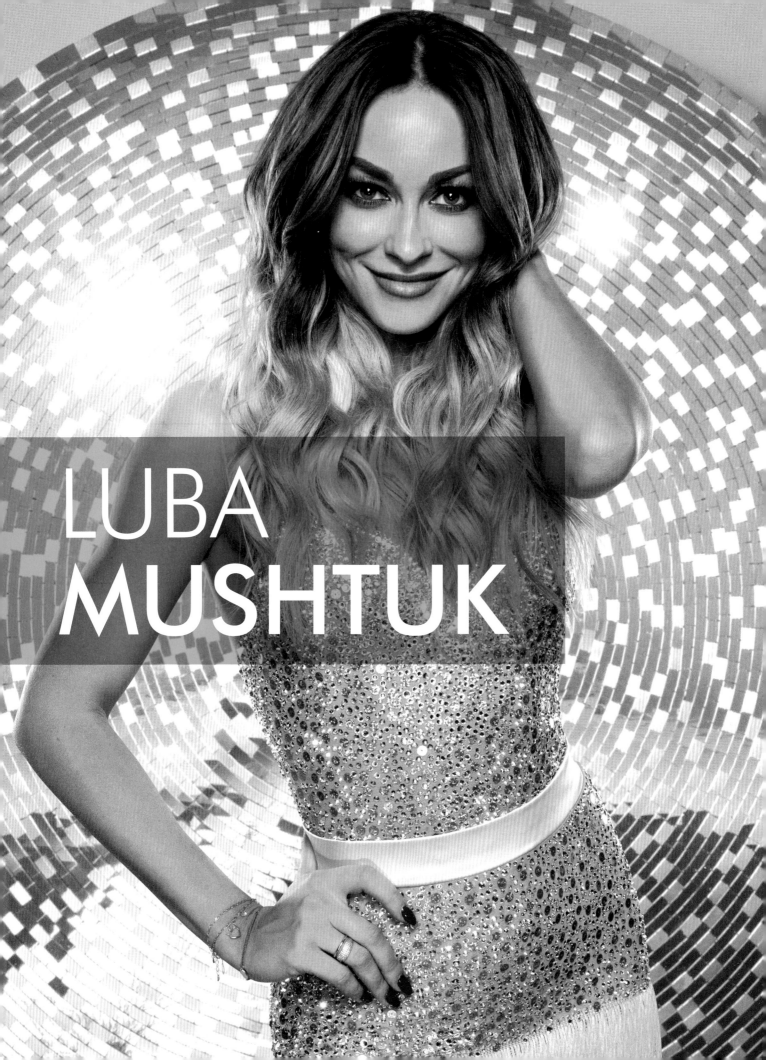

LUBA
MUSHTUK

ANSWERS

Spot the Difference, pages 30–31 • Find the Glitterball, pages 120–1